# THOUSAND SONS

## THE PSYCHIC SCOURGE

# CONTENTS

## PRODUCED BY GAMES WORKSHOP IN NOTTINGHAM

With thanks to the Mournival for their additional playtesting services

Games Workshop Ltd, Willow Rd, Lenton, Nottingham, NG7 2WS
**games-workshop.com**

# INTRODUCTION

Steel your mind against madness and horror, for you hold in your hands the definitive guide to Tzeentch's sorcerous Legion – the Thousand Sons. This tome will help you assemble your collection of Thousand Sons miniatures into a powerful tabletop army, ready to set the galaxy ablaze through arcane ritual and heretical wars.

The Thousand Sons are a Legion of sorcerers and spectral warriors, and are the most favoured mortal servants of the Chaos God Tzeentch – the Great Conspirator, the Architect of Fate, the Changer of the Ways. Driven by an undying desire for vengeance, as well as an insatiable lust for arcane power and daemonic knowledge, they launch their nightmarish wars against the forces of the Imperium. Whole swathes of realspace are left burning in their wake, yet each battle is but a single step in a larger plan, a lone ripple in the corrupted stream of fate.

With a wide array of ornately armoured warriors, daemonic war engines and mutated warp-creatures, the Thousand Sons offer any collector an exciting range of possibilities. The armies the Thousand Sons can field are as varied as the whims of Tzeentch himself, and whether you prefer elite cabals of sorcerers, heaving throngs of grotesque monstrosities or serried ranks of implacable automata, the Thousand Sons have the units and abilities to suit your needs.

Building and painting a Thousand Sons army is equally engaging. The miniatures in the range offer countless opportunities for any collector looking to create a distinctive aesthetic – ornate armour emblazoned with detailed runes featuring alongside mutated flesh and twisted machinery. Personalising your collection can be as simple as choosing the profane heraldry that your thrallband will bear to battle, or you can delve deep into the history of each of your warriors, with individualised mutations and different colours of warpflame enwreathing their weapons of war. The possibilities are limitless.

Within this book you will find all the information you need to collect a Thousand Sons army and field it upon the tabletop.

LEGION OF TZEENTCH: This section contains the history of the Thousand Sons, their fall to Chaos and their ongoing wars to twist the fate of the galaxy for the glory of Tzeentch. It also provides an in-depth analysis of how their armies organise themselves to fight.

AGENTS OF CHANGE: Here you will find a showcase of beautifully painted Citadel Miniatures that display the iconography and mutations of the Thousand Sons, as well as example armies to inspire your own collection.

WARRIORS OF LOST PROSPERO: This section includes datasheets, wargear lists and weapon rules for every Thousand Sons unit for use in your games.

SONS OF MAGNUS: This section provides additional rules – including Warlord Traits, Stratagems, Relics, psychic powers and matched play points – that allow you to transform your collection of Citadel Miniatures into an ensorcelled Thousand Sons army.

*To play games with your army, you will need a copy of the Warhammer 40,000 rules. To find out more about Warhammer 40,000 or download the free core rules, visit warhammer40000.com.*

With the might of a thousand psykers they breach the dam between reality and the immaterium, then come pouring forth to set worlds ablaze beneath their implacable march. A Legion shaped by the mutating energy of the warp, they are imbued with the sorcerous power of Tzeentch, and in his name they seek to transform the galaxy into a realm of nightmares and horror.

# LEGION OF TZEENTCH

**Wreathed in warpfire and imbued with boundless empyric energy, the Thousand Sons are the favoured mortal servants of Tzeentch, the Weaver of Destinies. What soul remains in these Heretic Astartes is consumed by a desire to see the Imperium burn.**

The air crackles with warp energy as the Thousand Sons make their approach. An aura of maddening flux radiates from the psychic core of the Traitor Legion, twisting hope into despair as the Chaos-bound warriors emerge onto the battlefield from tears in reality. As their warp presence flares even brighter, time shifts unnaturally, stretching seconds into seeming eternities and crushing minutes into fleeting moments. The only anchors to reality that remain are the racing heartbeats of the fearful and the incessant pounding of Rubric Marines advancing in perfect unison.

From the silently trudging ranks comes a hail of inferno bolts. These ensorcelled projectiles unleash the baleful energies of the immaterium upon impact, tearing through armour and riving flesh with ease. Even when the enemy returns fire, the Thousand Sons press on unabated. Salvoes of shots ricochet harmlessly off the Rubric Marines' ancient, ornate plating, and energy blasts dissipate in the warp fields that surround each Heretic Astartes. As the lifeless legionnaires draw closer to the enemy lines, torrents of warpflame are spewed forth, reducing all in their path to bubbling heaps of melted gore and slag. Beside them, Scarab Occult Terminators heft curved blades sheathed in shimmering power fields, cleaving effortlessly through any foes that dare obstruct their advance.

Enormous battle tanks and engines of war rumble alongside the Heretic Astartes, their corrupted machine spirits enslaved to the will of their dark masters. Rivulets of Chaos energy flow over their gleaming hulls, mutating metal plating into hideously twisted faces and screaming maws. Crushing the enemy's defences with sheer weight of firepower or beneath their adamantium tracks, the vehicles then unload more Rubric Marines from their transport bays to stride wordlessly into the carnage.

The incessant annihilation perpetrated by the Thousand Sons shifts to rapacious slaughter with the charge of savage herds of Tzaangors and teeming mobs of Chaos Cultists. As their onslaught gains momentum, the cacophony of inhuman braying and bellowed prayers is added to by blasts of rugged firearms and the revving of chainswords. Ignoring those in their number who fall to incoming fire, Tzeentch's footsoldiers hurl themselves bodily into combat, revelling in the transformations they work on their enemies' flesh with every hack and gouge.

The concentration of sorcery and the psychic agony of the dying pierces the veil between realspace and the warp, drawing forth Tzeentch's daemonic servants who eagerly leap into the fray. Horrors of varied hues spill through the ruptured membrane of reality, obliterating the minds of those they behold or simply incinerating them with spouts of coruscating flames. The skies fill with floating Flamers unleashing daemonic fire upon those below and flights of Screamers that swoop down with terrifying swiftness to shred the flesh of the living with their slashing talons.

The hellscape of the battlefield becomes even more nightmarish as twisted monstrosities neither natural nor daemonic emit soul-shredding howls. Chaos Spawn – shambling heaps of musculature, claws and jagged protrusions – barrel forwards to eviscerate their enemies with unthinking fury. Those unfortunate foes caught in the flux field emanating from Mutalith Vortex Beasts are ravaged by hideous mutations, their internal organs bursting outwards and their bodies contorting into paradoxical configurations. Fuelled by the unquenchable anguish of entombed Heretic Astartes, Helbrutes pulverise the packed ranks that stand before them, while Daemon Engines stomp and swoop across the battlefield, blasting apart enemy armour and crushing infantry beneath their massive frames.

*'Magnus the Red, the traitorous lord of the Thousand Sons, once more walks the Sea of Stars. He is a destroyer, a despoiler, a creature of ruin. He has brought his soulless Legion forth from the warp and wreathed them in Daemon fire. We know not how they will strike or the fell sorceries they will unleash, for it is impossible to know the mind of the Cyclops. Any man who says otherwise is a fool or a drunkard.'*

*- Logan Grimnar, High King of Fenris*

The majority of the Thousand Sons' warriors are walking relics – fusions of technology and sorcery that are devoid of fear or the capacity for reason. They are a Legion bound by dark and eldritch powers, soulless servants of Tzeentch who march implacably forwards to set the galaxy ablaze. Guiding the cults and thrallbands of the Thousand Sons are cabals of master psykers, Sorcerers and Daemon Princes who seek to twist the wending paths of destiny towards their own inscrutable ends, and above all these is the Daemon Primarch Magnus the Red. Every merciless onslaught launched is but a single step in a millennia-spanning stratagem, and each world turned into a blazing pyre is a single component in yet another unfathomable warp ritual.

For a hundred centuries the Thousand Sons have been a scourge to the Imperium of Man, their ruinous designs complex beyond mortal comprehension. The warpaths they carve through Imperial space are simultaneously destructive and subtle, both fluid and immutable. Though the Legion's Sorcerers and Daemon Princes are creatures of near-infinite ambition, their machinations ultimately serve the will of their Primarch and their god, whether intentionally or not.

Created by the Emperor as the fifteenth Legion of Adeptus Astartes, the Thousand Sons fell to the taint of Chaos during the Horus Heresy. Magnus was a peerless psyker, unmatched in power save by the Emperor himself. Through his gene-seed his psychic potential was passed on to the Space Marines in his Legion, along with a susceptibility to mutations of the flesh. Magnus saw Horus give himself to the Chaos Gods, and using his sorcerer's mind tried to warn the Emperor of the coming destruction. But this warning was not heeded, and Magnus was declared an outcast for using the powers of the warp so brazenly.

The Emperor sent his Space Wolves to bring the Thousand Sons to heel, but the Sons of Russ failed to silence Magnus and his sorcerous children. The XV Legion retreated from realspace, and in the warp the vast majority of their number were transformed into incorporeal automata. When they were next seen, the Thousand Sons fought at the side of Horus, wreaking vengeance on the warriors still loyal to the Emperor. Though Horus was ultimately slain, the Thousand Sons continue to fight in the Long War, and have waited patiently for the time of their emergence and retribution.

'They flee from the horrors I bring about; they fear the mutations I wreak on their flesh. Do they see beauty in the chaos I create? No. For Tzeentch has not opened their all-seeing eye.'

- Mordant Hex, Sorcerer Lord of the Six-Cursed

When the fleets of the Thousand Sons appear above a world, traditional defensive batteries are of limited use, for though the Sons of Magnus employ assault craft and drop-ships, they also possesses the power to tear passages in reality. This allows them to march their dreaded Rubricae from the halls of the Silver Towers directly onto the field of battle.

# SONS OF MAGNUS

**Before their fall to Chaos, the Thousand Sons were a Legion of warrior scholars, robust in body and mind. The gene-seed of their Primarch Magnus left them disposed to psychic mutations, but the Crimson King harnessed this flaw, fostering in his children a grasp of empyric powers unmatched throughout the Imperium.**

When the Primarchs were wrenched from their incubation pods on Terra and scattered across the galaxy, Magnus the Red fell upon the remote colony world of Prospero. Even as an infant he displayed an innate psychic ability which would have seen him butchered as a mutant on most planets in the Imperium. But this was not his destiny, for Prospero was a remote planet whose inhabitants had made it a refuge for psykers. It was into the communes of these outcasts that the child Primarch was accepted.

Magnus was made a ward of the scholars of Prospero, who viewed his comet-like arrival as a portent of his significance. They were not wrong in this view, for the crimson-skinned child quickly surpassed the abilities of the greatest adepts in the communes and achieved mastery over each of the psychic disciplines they studied. As he matured, Magnus grew into a giant, both mentally and physically, eventually coming to behold the vastness of the empyrean. He witnessed the incomprehensibility of the warp and from it drew much wisdom and knowledge. More than one consciousness saw the mind of Magnus also, shining like a bright beacon amongst the roil of Chaos. Chief among these was his distant sire, the Emperor of Mankind.

It is said that the psychic communion formed between the Emperor and Magnus was so strong that when the Emperor eventually came to Prospero at the head of a mighty warhost, he and Magnus greeted each other as old friends. The Emperor had chosen his XV Legion of Adeptus Astartes to be his vanguard force, for these were the progeny infused with Magnus' own gene-seed – the Thousand Sons. Magnus accepted command of this army before kneeling and swearing undying fealty to his Emperor.

The reunion of Magnus with his Legion was a great boon for the Thousand Sons. They were inheritors of their Primarch's mental and physical fortitude, but were also disposed to unstable psychic mutations. The rampant manifestation of psykers throughout their ranks had caused them to be feared and despised by many in the Imperium, with some calling for their complete eradication. Even amongst their fellow Space Marines, some viewed the Thousand Sons as a danger to Humanity – an entire Legion of potential mutants armed and armoured with Imperial technology. By relocating the Thousand Sons to Prospero, Magnus saved them from the witch hunts that sought to purge the Imperium of psykers. He then turned his colossal intellect towards instructing his gene-progeny in the ways of psychic mastery, training them to control the enormous power that lay within them.

Some scholars believe it was at this early stage that Magnus first entreated the Chaos Gods, sacrificing his right eye to these entities in exchange for the power to stabilise the mutations that ate at his Legion. Whether or not the threshold of sorcery was crossed at this time, Magnus fostered in the Thousand Sons some of the most potent Librarians of the epoch, and their might was terrifying to behold.

Joining the Great Crusade to reclaim the galaxy, Magnus and his Sons fought with vigour and tactical brilliance. Their campaigns were marked by deft feints and misdirection, shattering their enemies' defences with guile and trickery rather than brute force. Using psychic illusion to obscure their advances, the Thousand Sons impelled their foes to deploy too thinly across an embattled planet, or lured the main bulk of an opposing force off world so that the remaining soldiers could be effortlessly overrun. When they did engage the enemy, the Thousand Sons tended to avoid close combat, relying instead on ranged weaponry and devastating psychic assaults to secure victory. Xenos empires, enclaves of mutants and human populations who refused the dominion of the Emperor, all were consumed by the fires of Magnus and his Legion.

The powers employed by the Thousand Sons did not go unnoticed by the other Legiones Astartes. Battle-brothers witnessed their Prosperine allies tearing psychic maws in the skies above battlefields from which bolts of eldritch energy racked the enemy ranks. Alien war machines were pulverised by force of thought, and the flesh of the faithless was tortuously warped by will alone. Though Librarians of many Legions were possessed of similar psychic might, their abilities were disciplined,

carefully controlled and honed to be a tool of the Imperium. The wanton fashion in which the Thousand Sons wielded their psychic energies showed no such restraint, and the effects they achieved were far more terrifying.

Such powers had been seen in other places in the galaxy – in dark places the light of the Emperor had not yet reached. On worlds controlled by enclaves of heretics who openly worshipped unknown gods, warriors of the Great Crusade had felt the same unfettered psychic fury that they now saw used by Magnus' Legion. Once again, suspicion and mistrust loomed over the Thousand Sons, for even amongst other Imperial psykers they were seen as practitioners of the abhorrent. Their most vocal detractors were the sepulchral lord of the Death Guard, Mortarion, and the bellicose Primarch of the Space Wolves, Leman Russ. In the path Magnus had chosen for his Legion they saw only corruption, and their opposition to their brother threatened to sunder the very foundations of the Emperor's new order.

The regalia of the Thousand Sons has always borne elements of the Legion's Prosperine heritage, with scrolls, sigils and headdresses incorporated into their Imperial power armour. After their fall to Tzeentch, the Legion completely embraced their magi culture, and the ancient, arcane symbols of their destroyed home world that had once been merely vestiges became far more pronounced.

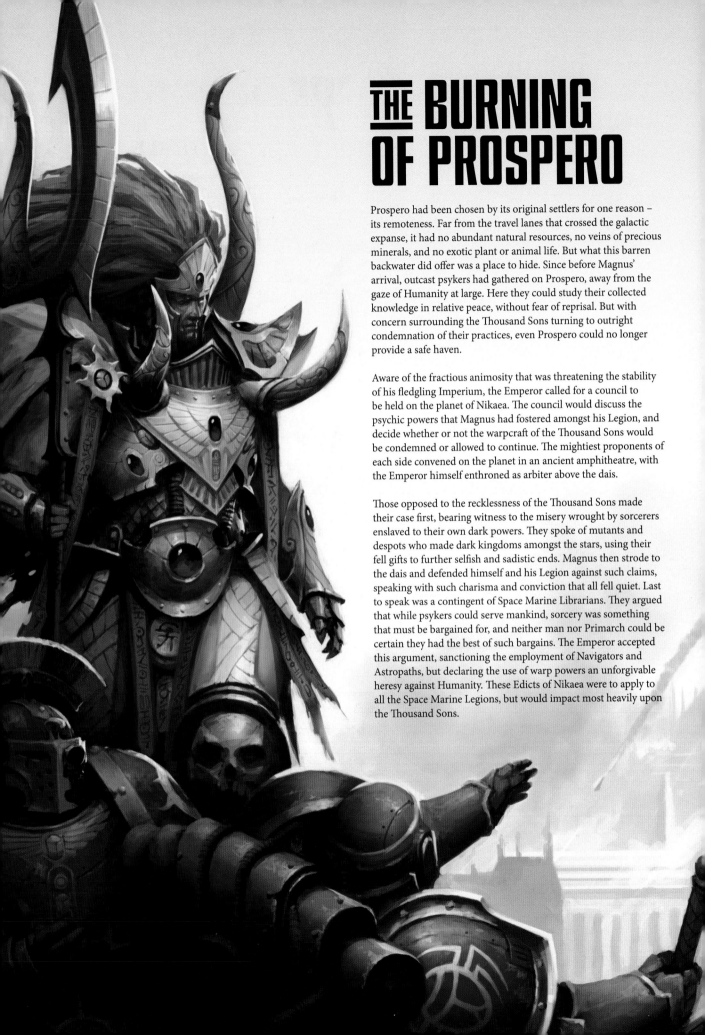

# THE BURNING OF PROSPERO

Prospero had been chosen by its original settlers for one reason – its remoteness. Far from the travel lanes that crossed the galactic expanse, it had no abundant natural resources, no veins of precious minerals, and no exotic plant or animal life. But what this barren backwater did offer was a place to hide. Since before Magnus' arrival, outcast psykers had gathered on Prospero, away from the gaze of Humanity at large. Here they could study their collected knowledge in relative peace, without fear of reprisal. But with concern surrounding the Thousand Sons turning to outright condemnation of their practices, even Prospero could no longer provide a safe haven.

Aware of the fractious animosity that was threatening the stability of his fledgling Imperium, the Emperor called for a council to be held on the planet of Nikaea. The council would discuss the psychic powers that Magnus had fostered amongst his Legion, and decide whether or not the warpcraft of the Thousand Sons would be condemned or allowed to continue. The mightiest proponents of each side convened on the planet in an ancient amphitheatre, with the Emperor himself enthroned as arbiter above the dais.

Those opposed to the recklessness of the Thousand Sons made their case first, bearing witness to the misery wrought by sorcerers enslaved to their own dark powers. They spoke of mutants and despots who made dark kingdoms amongst the stars, using their fell gifts to further selfish and sadistic ends. Magnus then strode to the dais and defended himself and his Legion against such claims, speaking with such charisma and conviction that all fell quiet. Last to speak was a contingent of Space Marine Librarians. They argued that while psykers could serve mankind, sorcery was something that must be bargained for, and neither man nor Primarch could be certain they had the best of such bargains. The Emperor accepted this argument, sanctioning the employment of Navigators and Astropaths, but declaring the use of warp powers an unforgivable heresy against Humanity. These Edicts of Nikaea were to apply to all the Space Marine Legions, but would impact most heavily upon the Thousand Sons.

As Magnus moved to storm from the hall, the Emperor himself stopped his son, and he bade Magnus cease his pursuit of arcane knowledge. This was not the outcome Magnus had wanted, and his crimson face was wan and brittle. Yet, as recorded in the Grimoire Hereticus, Magnus bowed before his Emperor and pledged loyalty and obeisance from himself and his Legion. Though none in attendance knew at that moment, this would be the last time that Magnus and the Emperor would meet.

Though the crisis was thought resolved at Nikaea, the fear surrounding sorcery had masked other, more insidious betrayals that would soon be unleashed upon the Imperium. On Davin, the Warmaster Horus fell to the dark manipulations of Chaos. The Primarch, once the right hand of the Emperor, was utterly enthralled by the baleful gods that dwelt within the warp, and emerged from that planet with a singular desire to see the galaxy burn. Along with his own Legion, other Primarchs were swayed to Horus' cause, joining their Legions to his mighty army and together plotting to take the Imperium, and even the Emperor, completely by surprise.

From his sanctum on Prospero, Magnus saw through the warp and beheld a vision of Horus' fall to Chaos. He saw the treachery of Angron and his World Eaters, of Fulgrim and the Emperor's Children. In that moment, the Crimson King was aware of the traps being laid for the Legions still loyal to the Emperor. The Iron Hands, the Salamanders and the Raven Guard would be laid low on Isstvan V. Guilliman's Ultramarines would be lured to the far side of the galaxy where they would be unable to defend against the horrors soon to unfold. The fate of the Imperium was known to Magnus. He alone perceived every event that would transpire and each role that would be played. Only his own place in this impending nightmare was unclear to him.

Aided by his fellow sorcerers, Magnus wove an immensely powerful spell that crossed time and space to breach the wards surrounding the Imperial Palace on Terra, and through this spell he cast a desperate message before the Emperor. The warning was not received as Magnus had hoped. Instead, the Emperor raged at Magnus' own betrayal. He had used forbidden sorcery, and in doing so had broken the seals that had protected the Imperial Palace. Rather than Horus, it was Magnus who was declared traitor. Utterly dismayed by his cyclopean son's actions, the Emperor broke psychic contact before Magnus' dire warning had even been conveyed.

The Emperor sent Leman Russ to lead an occupying force to Prospero and bring Magnus to justice. But Russ was deceived by Horus, whom he trusted and admired. With Horus' treachery still veiled, the Warmaster convinced Russ that the Emperor wished for him to execute Magnus and eradicate his Legion.

When the Space Wolves fleet arrived at Prospero they were completely unopposed. Some believe that their approach was masked by Tzeentch, where others claim it was the light of the Emperor that blinded the Thousand Sons to their attackers. Others still say that Magnus shielded the farseeing vision of his own sorcerers and prevented them from perceiving the coming Space Wolves, for in his despair he realised he had chosen the wrong path in his attempts to save the Imperium and now invited the retribution that would befall his world. Whatever the cause, the Space Wolves were able to bombard Prospero mercilessly. Fires raged across the planet's surface, consuming all that Magnus had created until only the capital city of Tizca remained.

As recorded in the Space Wolves saga, *The Edda of the Hammer*, the Fenrisian Legion landed on Prospero and made pyres of the tomes and relics the Thousand Sons held so dear. Magnus remained ensconced in his sanctum while the world around him burned, imploring his Legion to accept their deaths with honour. Ignoring these words, Ahzek Ahriman, Chief Librarian of the Thousand Sons, led a desperate defence of Tizca. Ahriman had ever viewed Magnus as a father and mentor, but this love was turned to ire by the Primarch's refusal to defend Prospero's last city. Despite Ahriman's efforts, the Thousand Sons were soon shattered, and Leman Russ – Horus' unwitting executioner – strode towards their lines, ready to butcher.

At last Magnus broke. Unable to bear the continued slaughter of his gene-children, he charged to meet Russ. The clash of Primarchs was more ferocious than all that had preceded it, with the cyclops battling the berserker right through the ruined heart of Tizca. It was Russ that eventually prevailed, snapping Magnus' back before raising his frost blade Mjalnar to deliver the finishing strike. But with a whispered word of power Magnus was spirited away before death could claim him and sent drifting through the warp. There he saw the salvation that had eluded him – he beheld sorcery incarnate, and with inextricable finality Magnus the Red forsook his Emperor and gave himself fully to the Dark God Tzeentch. In that instant, Tizca and the Thousand Sons vanished from the face of Prospero.

# THE RUBRIC OF AHRIMAN

As Horus' betrayal was finally revealed the Imperium was consumed by chaos, and that which Magnus had foreseen in his vision came to pass. Angron and Fulgrim joined in the Warmaster's treachery, as did Mortarion, who had once decried Magnus' sorcery as heretical. Together with these fallen Primarchs, the Warmaster established a stronghold on Isstvan V. Seven Space Marine Legions were sent to scour the traitors from the galaxy, but four of these had also fallen to the taint of Chaos, and sided with Horus. The Iron Hands, the Salamanders and the Raven Guard were massacred by their erstwhile brethren, and through the warp Magnus watched them die for a second time.

When the Thousand Sons emerged from the empyrean they too fought alongside the Warmaster, though the exact nature and extent of their involvement in the Horus Heresy is still unknown. What accounts exist of that dark time are closely guarded, and those regarding the Thousand Sons in particular are riddled with contradiction and paradox. What is known beyond doubt is that they unleashed their full psychic fury, wreaking vengeance on the Imperium that had declared them abominable and destroyed their world.

Also recorded is that the Thousand Sons joined the final siege on Terra, where the Horus Heresy reached its apocalyptic zenith. The Sons of Magnus descended upon the Imperial Palace with their fellow Traitors and slaughtered the defenders, shredding their ranks with incessant hails of bolt-fire and using their fell powers to fuse mortal flesh into twisted creatures of Chaos. Sorcerous cabals sundered the wards protecting the deepest Terran Librariums, allowing the Thousand Sons to plunder the relics and tomes housed within. But when Horus was slain at the Emperor's hand, the Chaos invasion was broken. The Thousand Sons and their heretical brethren fled into the gaping warp maw known as the Eye of Terror.

Horrendous mutations tore through most of the Traitor Legions as the warp was made manifest in their bodies and wargear. Limbs grew into cruelly clawed appendages, gun muzzles bristled with jagged teeth and Imperial aquilas morphed into the wretched symbols of the Chaos Gods. But at first the Thousand Sons were spared from this fate. Though their gene-seed had ever been unstable, they were shielded from metamorphoses by their new master, Tzeentch. Their patron god even guided the Legion to a new planet, deep within the Eye of Terror and rich in occult power. Here, on the Planet of the Sorcerers, the Sons of Magnus believed they would find a haven within the warp where they could continue their arcane studies. But the God of Change is ever capricious.

No sooner had the Thousand Sons claimed dominion over their new home world than they too were afflicted by the grotesque transfigurations of Chaos. The flesh-change

– known and feared since the Legion's founding – came swift and unsparingly, reshaping their bodies into inextricable forms more pleasing to the twisted eye of Tzeentch. This was followed by despair, for the long and exacting pursuit of knowledge had resulted in the very abomination the Thousand Sons had sought to overcome.

When their armour is punctured by bolt or blade, the dust of the Rubricae pours out. And yet it is from this dust that the Rubricae can be given animus again – not life, but a ghostly simulacrum, devoid of thought or passion, and capable of great destruction.

> 'ECHOES OF THE PSYCHIC SCREAM WERE HEARD ACROSS THE ENTIRE IMPERIUM. SCORES OF ASTROPATHIC CHOIRS FELT A TERRIFYING POWER EMANATING FROM A SINGLE POINT IN THE WARP. THE MINDS OF MANY SANCTIONED PSYKERS WHO HAD BEEN TASKED WITH LISTENING FOR WHISPERS OF THE THOUSAND SONS WERE DEVOURED IN AN INSTANT, AND FROM THEIR RUPTURED BODIES AROSE CACKLING TZEENTCHIAN DAEMONS. ONLY NINE SURVIVED TO TELL OF WHAT THEY SAW.'
>
> *- On the Rubric of Ahriman, from the Grimoire Hereticus*

At this time Ahriman gathered to his side a cabal of the Legion's mightiest Sorcerers, and together they determined to undo the corruption of the flesh-change. They knew that Magnus would oppose their actions, and so Ahriman created wards of secrecy, under the cover of which his cabal's workings would go unseen. Hidden from view, they wove their mighty spell, then unleashed their creation across the Planet of the Sorcerers.

The Grimoire Hereticus records the moment that the Rubric of Ahriman was unveiled – a roar of anguished unreality flared within the warp, a maelstrom within the maelstrom of Chaos so unimaginably powerful that even Daemons fled from its upheaval. The skies on the Planet of the Sorcerers were enveloped by iridescent storms and torn by streaks of polychromatic lightning, with each bolt arcing down to strike one of the corrupted Thousand Sons. It was Magnus that eventually ceased this eruption of cosmic energy, calling upon the power of Tzeentch to halt Ahriman's sorcery. But the vast majority of the Legion had already been touched by the Rubric. Those struck had indeed been stripped of their mutations, for their flesh had been reduced to dust, mystically sealed inside their ensorcelled armour for eternity.

A second howl echoed through the warp as Magnus beheld his warrior sons. The once-enlightened scholars of Prospero now stood as soulless automata on the surface of a Daemon world. Everything the Crimson King had worked for and each sacrifice he had made was now rendered useless, for he had failed to save his Legion from irrevocable damnation.

Filled with wrath, Magnus sought out Ahriman and his cabal, shattering the wards behind which the malefactors hid.

But Ahriman was defiant, claiming that the Rubric had achieved its ultimate goal in purging the Thousand Sons of mutation. As Magnus prepared to obliterate his most wayward son, the lord of both intervened. Tzeentch had plans yet for Ahriman, and so Magnus was compelled to banish him instead. The Primarch then ascended his tower and cast his baleful gaze upon the universe. With his home world destroyed, his father a sworn enemy and his Legion a spectral shadow of their former glory, Magnus vowed to see the galaxy burn.

# THE
# PLANET OF THE SORCERERS

**For ten thousand years the Planet of the Sorcerers has been the staging ground from which the Thousand Sons have launched their raids into realspace. A nightmarish world of Daemons, it was nested deep within the warp until by Magnus' hand it was drawn through the veil and thrust into the Emperor's domain.**

Whether the Planet of the Sorcerers has a natural origin or is merely a by-product of Tzeentch's will, none can say. It is a warped and twisted place, even compared to the worlds of other Traitor Legions – a locus of Chaos energy that the Thousand Sons use to fuel their diabolical craft. While it existed within the warp it orbited a constantly changing sun, an erratic orb that passed through nine distinct waxing and waning phases. The world itself is dark, rocky and violently volcanic. Leaden skies are riven by unholy power, and kaleidoscopic lightning illuminates the skyline with impossible hues. Clouds of aetheric vapour release deluges of liquefied warp energy, which flow out to the seas that lie between the planet's vast, shifting continents.

Though the Planet of the Sorcerers is anathema to natural life, its surface is rife with Tzeentch's warp-spawned children, whose hideous screams fill the air as they coalesce into existence and disperse again. Other strange beings also manage to cling to a wretched existence among the erupting peaks and flux plains. Tzaangors – horrendous hybrids of beast, bird and man – roam the wastelands in nomadic warbands. Enormous monstrosities march beneath raging empyric storms leaving wide wakes of devastation. Most nightmarish are the shambling Chaos Spawn, fleshy amalgams of living creatures and raw Chaos energy.

The only place bearing any semblance of order on this constantly mutating planet is Tizca, the capital city of the Thousand Sons that was transported through the warp in its entirety from the devastated world of Prospero. The majestic spires that once lined the city have been replaced with disfigured obelisks that meld into the bedrock. The mighty pyramids of old have given way to mounds of crystalline earth-matter, and pillars of molten stone that pupate into metamorphic towers. These grotesque structures

house the halls of the Thousand Sons. Inside them lies the dark lore the Traitor Legion has harvested over its long existence, stored in endless rows of profane librariums whose walls pulsate and echo with daemonic wailing. Those mortals brought inside the sanctums are flensed of their sanity by the raw psychic resonance, preparing them perfectly for the Thousand Sons' sorcerous experimentations.

Many are the malshapen edifices of Tizca, but they are all dwarfed by the innermost megalith – the Tower of the Cyclops. Looming ominously over the planet's surface, its highest levels contain Magnus' personal sanctum, and from the pinnacle comes a flood of iridescent light, cast by an entrapped tempest of glowing warp energy. This raging storm is enveloped by an orb of profane wards, and through the eye of the storm Magnus watches the manifold paths of the past, present and future. For thousands of years Magnus has observed the material universe from his tower, biding his time and planning his master strokes of avengement.

Yet the Planet of the Sorcerers is not merely a secluded refuge in which the Thousand Sons toil at their dark arts; it is a base of warfare, a staging ground for campaigns of annihilation that are waged against the Imperium of Man. Tizca is replete with labyrinthine armouries that contain racks upon racks of warp-infused weaponry.

Corrupted manufactorums – either gifted from the Dark Mechanicum or wrenched through the warp from incinerated forge worlds – belch smoke into the auroral atmosphere as they churn out waves of daemonic siege engines. Between the twisting forms of the buildings themselves are enormous mustering grounds ringed by inscrutable Tzeentchian runes. Here the rows of Rubricae are gathered, ready to be marched into the corridors of the awaiting Silver Towers. From there they are unleashed upon the unforgiven enemies of the Sorcerer-Lords.

The catastrophic effects of a full-scale Thousand Sons invasion are exemplified by the Legion's attack on the Fenris System. The attack drew the Space Wolves back to defend their home world, allowing the Sons of Magnus to wreak vengeance upon them. Unnatural footsoldiers from the entire Chaos pantheon joined in the slaughter before Magnus himself stepped forth from the warp onto the surface of Fenris, there to face the Chapter that had thought to execute his sons on Prospero. Space Wolves, Dark Angels and Grey Knights champions fell to Magnus' psychic might, their minds and bodies dashed to particulate matter. But the Great Wolf Logan Grimnar was able to land a blow on the Crimson King, allowing the Daemon hunters of the Grey Knights to work their rites of banishment. Though the invasion was driven back, its purpose had been achieved. The psychic anguish of a billion deaths rippled through the immaterium, providing the final component in a ritual millennia in the making. The power taken from the worlds of the Space Wolves saturated the Planet of the Sorcerers. It vanished from the warp only to burst violently into realspace, appearing near the burnt husk of Prospero. The old and new home worlds of the Thousand Sons now orbit the same cursed star – a star that has become an omen of doom in the skies throughout the Imperium.

## THE WARP FLEETS OF MAGNUS

Scarring the minds of all who look upon them, the Silver Towers are the largest remnants of ancient Prospero's citadel spires. Each of these mighty fortresses exists across dimensions, and wherever they go they spread the chaotic influence of Tzeentch. Though they manifest in realspace, the Silver Towers contain chambers that are fragments of the Crystal Labyrinth entwining the Grand Conspirator's Realm. For millennia the Silver Towers have been harbingers of madness and death, appearing from warp fractures above Imperial worlds across the galaxy. Arcane lightning lances out to incinerate anything that draws near to them while cruelly mawed cannons and more esoteric weapons open fire. When the gates of the Silver Towers open, rank upon rank of Thousand Sons march forth to enact destruction.

Magnus leads his warp fleets from his flagship, *Tizca's Revenge*. This vast and monstrous craft is fashioned from the plundered resources of an entire Imperial world, fused together with unfathomable warp energies as a simulacrum of the Great Pyramid of Tizca.

# CULTS OF THE THOUSAND SONS

After the Rubric of Ahriman, the confluence of once noble fellowships that comprised the Legion was replaced by a hierarchy born of Magnus' will. The Thousand Sons were divided into nine great cults, each devoted to a separate facet of the Change God, and whether wittingly or not these cults all serve Magnus, and all have a purpose in the unfathomable plans of Tzeentch.

Though the Planet of the Sorcerers is a world in constant flux, its inhabitants are governed by a strict order set in place by Magnus. The spectral remnants of the Legion's warriors, known as the Rubricae, reign over throngs of Cultists, Tzaangors and mutated warp beasts, while above the Rubricae is the former bodyguard of the Crimson King, known as the Sekhmet. Raised above all of these is the Rehati – a coven of nine Exalted Sorcerers and Daemon Princes who are favoured by Tzeentch more than any other amongst the Thousand Sons, save Magnus himself.

From this overarching hierarchy, the Legion's forces are further divided into nine great cults. At the head of each is a member of the Rehati who bears the ancient rank of Magister Templi. Beneath each Magister Templi are nine other Daemon Princes and Sorcerers who, though lesser in rank, still bear much of Tzeentch's favour. These nine steer the cult along the ever-changing paths of fate. Other Sorcerers hold lower positions in the cult, and along with troops, tanks, mutants and Daemon Engines are capable of claiming vast swathes of realspace for their cult masters. Each cult has worlds from which they draw resources and magical energy, and populous planets to provide them with constant streams of Cultist soldiers, slaves and subjects for their arcane experiments.

Aside from constituting a terrifying military force, each of the cults is an amalgam of the twisted minds of those in its ranks, and though inherently self-serving, the members of a given cult are ultimately bent towards the same purpose. To a mortal mind, untouched by Tzeentch's corruptions, the complex plans laid out by these cults are utterly unfathomable, but to the Thousand Sons they are both a form of profane worship and a route to vengeance over the Imperium. Often, the goals of a given cult will undermine or even contradict those of the other cults. As such, the cults are wary of one another, and alliances between them are ever shifting. The power and influence of each is also in constant flux, with every cult going through cycles of activity and torpidity as befits their inscrutable machinations.

It is extremely rare for the entirety of a cult to deploy in a single war zone, though when this does happen the fabric of reality quakes in their presence. More often, the cult's malevolent goals require its forces to be spread throughout space and time, allowing each splinter to play a separate role in some larger and more sinister stratagem. A cult therefore comprises many sects, each of which may prosecute their own seemingly unconnected campaigns of terror. Where the combined forces of a cult could easily set a whole system ablaze, a single sect is still capable of devastating a planet. Often, several sects will launch simultaneous strikes across large tracts of realspace, plunging entire sub-sectors into disarray and panic. As nearby worlds send reinforcements to the embattled planets, more Thousand Sons appear to attack where defences have been stretched to breaking point. Devastating as they are, these attacks rarely give any clue as to the ultimate goals of the cult.

A sect is made up of multiple thrallbands, which can also act independently of each other. With several units of Thousand Sons bolstered by auxiliary troops and vehicles, a single thrallband can obliterate an enemy fortress or turn a city into a blazing pyre. A number of thrallbands operate in complete isolation – some have been exiled from the Planet of the Sorcerers, while others chose to leave to pursue their own ends. But even these forces ultimately serve the goals of one of the nine cults, whether they themselves know it or not.

## THE NINE CULTS

The Cult of Prophecy is guided by incessant whispers that bleed from the warp. From these they divine the outcomes of multiple futures, and seek out events that can be twisted to their own purpose.

The Cult of Time is similarly enthralled by the future, as well as the present and past. They view the flow of time as an unwrought resource that can be shaped into a weapon. By their victories, ripples are sent both forwards and backwards in time, so that their enemies may be defeated before they are even engaged.

The Cult of Mutation embodies the transfiguring aspect of Tzeentch. Not only do they embrace the warping of flesh, but also the warping of reality itself. By their hand civilised planets are transformed into Daemon worlds, and entire populations moulded into grotesque abominations.

The Cult of Scheming is perhaps the most insidious of the cults, for the creation of convoluted plots is to them a form of profane worship. Every conquest and withdrawal is a perfectly planned manoeuvre, a single step that leads towards some unseen master stroke.

The Cult of Magic is dedicated to the pure and unfettered use of sorcery. Their bloody campaigns are launched to secure arcane objects held by Imperial, xenos and other Chaos forces. These artefacts are then used as foci in the weaving of devastating spells.

The Cult of Knowledge is also drawn to the many curios hidden throughout the galaxy, particularly tomes of eldritch learnings, dark secrets and paradoxical logics. Through such lore, the cult is able to extrapolate the weaknesses in their enemies, and in the fabric of reality itself.

The Cult of Change is anathema to order. They are the great unravellers, launching their armies wherever civilisation and reason exist. Similarly, in places of utter anarchy, the cult appears to impose their ever-shifting will.

The Cult of Duplicity is unique within the Legion in that it both is and is not guided by a unified desire. The Sorcerers of this cult are by their very nature deceivers, at once appearing fractured and singular in their purpose. As such, it is impossible to know whether the sects within the cult are acting independently or as part of a singular, terrifying plan.

The Cult of Manipulation is similarly deceptive, using its tendrillar web of influence to sway the actions of its enemies. Vast networks of mortal and daemonic spies allow the cult to oversee their plots as they unfold through assassination, possession and the wreaking of pure havoc.

# LEGION ORGANISATION

By the will of Magnus the Red, the Thousand Sons Legion is divided into nine cults – twisted mockeries of the nine noble fellowships of Prospero. Each cult has hundreds of Sorcerers who guide thousands of Rubricae warriors to war, and though the relative power of each cult may wax or wane, nine there shall always be, for nine is the number of Tzeentch.

*The nine fellowships of the Thousand Sons Legion have become cults dedicated to furthering Tzeentch's plots across time and space.*

## CULT OF MAGIC

**CULT COMMAND**
**Magister Templi**
Exalted Sorcerer

**Magister Templi Retinue**
Familiars, Acolytes and Bodyguards

**Cult Assets**
- Cult Flagship
- Silver Tower Constellations
- Battleships
- Escort Squadrons
- Summoned Daemon Cohorts
- Sorcerer Thrallbands
- Super-heavy Squadrons

| CULT OF SCHEMING | CULT OF MANIPULATION | CULT OF TIME |
|---|---|---|

*Sects are identified by their livery and the sigils they use to mark their armour. Each consists of a number of thrallbands, as the warbands of Thousand Sons sorcerer-champions are called, themselves marked with runic combinations favoured by their Magister.*

| 1st Sect | 2nd Sect | 3rd Sect | 4th Sect |
|---|---|---|---|

| 1st Thrallband | 3rd Thrallband |
|---|---|

## 2nd Thrallband

Thrallbands consist of nine lesser Sorcerer Thralls under the command of a Magister, who is a Sorcerer, Exalted Sorcerer or Daemon Prince.

Each Magister is an architect of war, leading his thrallband in their campaigns of ruination. Beneath his command are nine lesser magi, Sorcerers who serve as his chief advisors and battlefield lieutenants.

**Thrallband Assets**
- Helbrutes
- Daemon Engines
- Battle Tanks
- Transport Vehicles
- Chaos Cultists
- Tzaangors
- Chaos Spawn

MAGISTER
1 Exalted Sorcerer

Lesser Sorcerers

## LEGION COMMAND
**Magnus the Red, Daemon Primarch of Tzeentch**

**Rehati**
Daemon Princes and Exalted Sorcerers of Tzeentch

**Sekhmet Conclave**
Scarab Occult Terminator Formations

**Legion Assets**
- Daemon World Planetary Domains
- The Tower of the Cyclops
- Legion Flagship
- Capital-class Warships
- Secondary Escort Squadrons
- Space Hulks
- Bound Greater Daemons
- Legion Armorium
- Vassal Renegade Chapter Warbands
- Auxiliary Forces

| CULT OF KNOWLEDGE | CULT OF CHANGE | CULT OF DUPLICITY | CULT OF MUTATION | CULT OF PROPHECY |

## 6TH SECT

**SECT COMMAND**
**Arch Magister**
Exalted Sorcerer

**Arch Magister Retinue**
Familiars, Acolytes and Bodyguards

**Sect Assets**
- Silver Towers
- Escorts
- Planetary Assault Craft and Drop-ships
- Daemon Engine Packs
- Cultist Covens
- Tzaangor Warherds
- Super-heavy Assets

| 5TH SECT | | 6TH SECT |

| 4th Thrallband | 5th Thrallband | 6th Thrallband |

Beneath the Magister and his favoured Sorcerers are lesser thralls – Aspiring Sorcerers and Scarab Occult Sorcerers who direct the ranks of lifeless Rubricae and Scarab Occult Terminators.

3 squads of Rubric Marines, each led by an Aspiring Sorcerer

3 squads of Scarab Occult Terminators, each led by a Scarab Occult Sorcerer

# HOSTS OF THE PSYKER LORDS

The Thousand Sons are known not only for their intricate battle stratagems and the destructive sorceries they unleash upon their enemies. Their armour and heraldry is also instantly recognisable, and the Legion marches to war bearing the symbols of their Prosperine heritage alongside runes and sigils devoted to Tzeentch.

Aside from the slavering throngs of Cultists and Tzaangors, the bulk of a Thousand Sons thrallband is composed of Rubric Marines. These warriors tower over mortal humans on the battlefield, and with lifeless, warp-driven movements they march inexorably through all but the most punishing fire. Their armour is irreplaceable, for each suit was fused with the essence of the warrior inside by the Rubric of Ahriman. However, any given Rubric Marine may have been felled in battle dozens or even hundreds of times, his essence inevitably restored once again to his armour by a sorcerous master to fight in another campaign of horror. As such, the armour of the Rubricae is both a grim reminder of the devastation done unto the Legion, and the means by which the Thousand Sons wreak their vengeance upon the Imperium of Man.

The Rubricae in a given thrallband – along with the Sorcerers and Sekhmet warriors who march to battle with them – are all adorned in the colours and symbols of their Magister, with additional iconography on the armour and tabard. These icons have various and often simultaneous meanings, with some denoting the Aspiring Sorcerer to whom a Rubric Marine is enthralled, and others recording a lost piece of Prosperine lore.

## SORCEROUS ICONOGRAPHY

The symbols of Tzeentch and Magnus the Red are displayed boldly on the armour of the Thousand Sons. In addition, these symbols are sometimes wrought in warp-drenched metal and held aloft by a Rubric Marine, allowing the flickering flames of Tzeentch to lap at the enemy.

The Legion's sigil – or one of its many variants – is typically displayed on the left pauldron. This symbol shows the fiery drake devouring its own tail.

The right pauldron is usually emblazoned with the iconography of a warrior's sect. These symbols are multifarious in their shape and meaning, with some mirroring the symbol of Tzeentch, others the eye of Magnus, and others still some long-forgotten Prosperine icon.

As befits the servants of Tzeentch, the Thousand Sons have changed greatly in appearance since the days before the Horus Heresy. Where they once wore crimson, the manifold sects now decorate their armour with innumerable hues. Blues, yellows and golds are favoured, but many other colours are seen in their garb and sigils, particularly those that are believed to have some past or future significance. Each sect is unified in its colours and heraldry, with individual thrallbands also bearing their own unique insignias.

## THE TIZCAN HOST

The Tizcan Host is known for its shared delusion of attaining perfect purity through the Rubric of Ahriman. They are devout adherents of the Cult of Magic, and their thrallbands are perhaps the most warlike of any amongst the Legion. They announce their presence on the battlefield with bombardments of iridescent warp energy.

Khar en Shaphat of the Cleansed Ninefold

## SECT OF THE RED ECHO

Though their leaders were once known for their forbearance, the Sect of the Red Echo has carved a gruesome warpath since falling to Tzeentch, with haunting screams following wherever they go. Some amongst the Cult of Time interpret these as the dying cries of their victims, others as the mad harmonies of the warp itself.

Farroteth of the Silent Scream

## THE CRYSTAL HARBINGERS

The Sorcerers of the Crystal Harbingers delve into the hidden recesses of the Silver Towers to explore the Tzeentchian labyrinth to which they lead. Here they glean portents of the future and commune with daemonic entities, which they then use to terrifying effect in their wars against the forces of the Imperium.

Amyr Vasser Suhk of the Fractal Barons

## THE HERMETIC BLADES

As a sub-sect of the Cult of Mutation, the Grand Order of the Hermetic Blades view flesh as a twisted cage that imprisons the soul. Their numerous close-combat warriors are charged with taking battlefield captives who are brought back to the Planet of the Sorcerers, there to be used in gruesome soul-flaying experiments.

Khamonaht the Lacerater of the Knights of Emancipation

## THE PRISM OF FATE

The Prism of Fate has always prided itself on the diversity of psychic manifestations that have been mastered amongst its ranks, as well as the variety of ways in which these warp powers can inflict death. The sect's Sorcerers are quick to unleash new forms of devastation upon their enemies, making them exemplars amongst the Cult of Change.

*Omarion Ragaar of the Refracted Sons*

## BLADES OF MAGNUS

The Blades of Magnus were long bound to the Cult of Manipulation, and worked in secret to break the bonds between Magnus and the eldritch powers. When the Daemon Primarch learned of their works he annihilated their minds with an overwhelming psychic blast. Now they are some of his most loyal thralls, replete with Rubric Marines.

*Ahmokhat the Cruel of the Third Order of Blades*

## THE CRIMSON SONS

In the wake of the Rubric of Ahriman, the Crimson Sons were exiled from the Planet of the Sorcerers, and have wrought mayhem in isolation from the main body of the Thousand Sons ever since. Like so many sects in the Cult of Duplicity, how their actions ultimately serve the will of Magnus is unknown to all but the Crimson King.

*Kairophon the Second of the Blooded Brotherhood*

## WARP GHEISTS

The white on the Warp Gheists' armour represents the bone remnants contained within. Their former Arch Magister, Nezchad Aratos, enacted a ritual to restore a portion of his exiled brethren's form, though he himself was destroyed by the spell. The sect has scoured the galaxy ever since in search of similarly powerful magics.

*Hocchad Zephek of the Teeth of Aratos*

---

Representations of the numbers one to ten in the ancient Prosperine script are employed to denote squad numbers within a thrallband. These numbers are typically displayed on a warrior or Sorcerer's tabard.

| 1 | 2 | 3 | 4 | 5 | 6 | 7 | 8 | 9 | 10 |
|---|---|---|---|---|---|---|---|---|----|

## THE REFLECTED ONES

The Sorcerers of the Reflected Ones view realspace as an imperfect mirroring of the warp, and seek to scour the galaxy of its impurities by weaving world-spanning mutagenic spells. The ranks of their enemies devolve into Chaos Spawn and braying Tzaangor herds before the Thousand Sons even set foot on the battlefield.

*Nebunak Surrian of the Twisted Visage*

## THRALLS OF MAGNUS

The Thralls of Magnus are the largest and most powerful sect of the Cult of Scheming, and have been since shortly after the Legion's fall. Many rival sects have sought to dethrone them, only to succumb to impossibly intricate traps and complots. The same inescapable fate has befallen countless Imperial and xenos worlds.

*Belkizadek eht Ra of the Makers of Truth*

## THE SILVER SONS

The Silver Sons covet certain priceless metals found within celestial objects, believing them to be links to the past and future. Once obtained, these metals are used in the creation of twisted Daemon Engines, and should such substances lie on inhabited worlds, the Silver Sons will incinerate all who stand between them and their prize.

*Oklithyon Duhk of the Nova-Born*

## THE SECTAI PROSPERINE

Originally a gathering of minor sects from the fringes of the Thousand Sons' hierarchy, the Sectai Prosperine now wield truly terrifying influence and power. They embrace their Legion's legacy, believing the dark fate of Prospero to have been a rare gift that imparted to them knowledge that would otherwise have remained hidden.

*Dramendesha the Lowborn of the Encircling Hex*

Many symbols are emblazoned on the armour of the Thousand Sons. These icons may denote the thrallband within a sect to which a warrior belongs, or the rank of a Sorcerer below their Magister. Other symbols have meanings that are closely guarded, known only to the Arch Magister of a sect or the Magister Templi of a cult.

# CONFLAGRATION OF WAR

Though the Thousand Sons have ever been a peril to the Imperium, now more than ever they threaten to burn the galaxy to cinders. Perhaps most horrifying is the notion that their campaigns of destruction may be designed merely to distract from or veil their grander machinations.

HALO STARS

SCARUS SECTOR

## SEGMENTUM OBSCURUS

NAOGEDDON

DIMMAMAR

STORM OF THE EMPEROR'S WRATH

CALIXIS SECTOR

FINIAL SECTOR

CYPRA MUNDI

GOTHIC SECTOR

**3**

ERROR: UNVERIFIED NAV-DATA **8**

MORDIAN

VALHALLA

THE EYE OF TERROR

NACHMUND GAUNTLET

BELIS CORONA

PISCINA

ALARIC

BAAL

CHINCHARE

CADIA

IMPERIUM

AGRIPINAA

FENRIS

MOLOV

**1**

CICATRIX MALEDICTUM

HYDRAPHUR

ARMAGEDDON

ELYSIA

**2**

## SEGMENTUM SOLAR

LASTRATI

VORDRAST

Prospero & Planet of the Sorcerers

GOLGOTHA

SEGMENTUM PACIFICUS

TERRA & MARS

RYZA

**5**

ERROR: UNVERIFIED NAV-DATA **8**

GATHALAMOR

CATACHAN

THE MAELSTROM

**7**

NECROMUNDA

**8**

MACHARIA

BADAB

ULTIMA MACHARIA

KRIEG

LUTHER MCINTYRE

TALLARN

CHIROS

OPHELIA

NOCTURNE

BALOR

UHULIS SECTOR

V'RUN

SIREN'S STORM

ALEUSIS

SOLSTICE

RYNN'S WORLD

BANE'S LANDING

## SEGMENTUM TEMPESTUS

REDUCTUS SECTOR

AGRAX

NEPHILIM SECTOR

BAKKA

ANTAGONIS

SAN LEOR

GRYPHONNE IV

Item number: 2G27.63–759. Star chart fragments intercepted by the Astra Telepathica and compiled for Logan Grimnar.

ILLUSTRIS

THE VEILED REGION

ERROR: UNVERIFIED NAV-DATA **8**

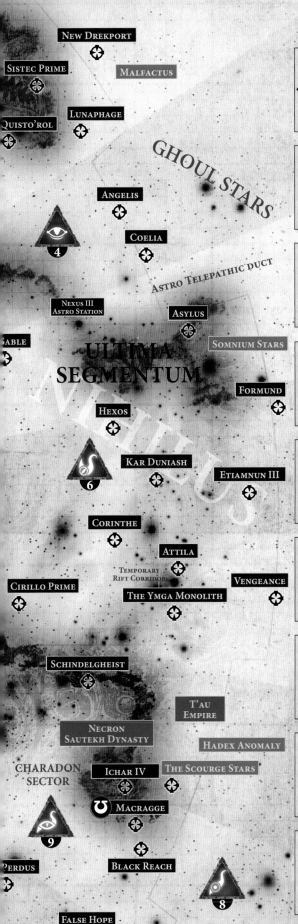

NEW DREKPORT

SISTEC PRIME

MALFACTUS

LUNAPHAGE

QUISTO'ROL

GHOUL STARS

ANGELIS

COELIA

4

ASTRO TELEPATHIC DUCT

ULTIMA SEGMENTUM

NEXUS III ASTRO STATION

ASYLUS

SOMNIUM STARS

...ABLE

NIHILUS

FORMUND

HEXOS

6

KAR DUNIASH

ETIAMNUN III

CORINTHE

ATTILA

TEMPORARY RIFT CORRIDORS

CIRILLO PRIME

THE YMGA MONOLITH

VENGEANCE

SCHINDELGHEIST

T'AU EMPIRE

NECRON SAUTEKH DYNASTY

HADEX ANOMALY

CHARADON SECTOR

ICHAR IV

THE SCOURGE STARS

9

MACRAGGE

...PERDUS

BLACK REACH

8

FALSE HOPE

SALEM

---

### 1. Cult of Prophecy – Nightmares Undreamt

As the beleaguered Imperial defenders of the Cadian Gate continue to be butchered, the Cult of Prophecy has begun a massive ritual of summoning around the Eye of Terror.

### 2. Cult of Time – Enslaving the Ancients

In their wars against the Necrons of the Nephrekh Dynasty, the Sorcerers of the Cult of Time seek to uncover the methods by which the star gods known as the C'tan were made slaves.

### 3. Cult of Mutation – Slash and Burn

The Ferric Blight ravages Kantakkha to the delight of the Plague God Nurgle's followers. But lattices of flaming glass have started to sprout, mutating the metallic rot into a crystalline labyrinth.

### 4. Cult of Scheming – Coming of the Despoilers

Deep within the Imperium Nihilus, sects from the Cult of Scheming terrorise the now isolated shrine worlds, prising the relics they seek from the charred hands of their defenders.

### 5. Cult of Magic – The Scintillating Straits

As Imperial fleets try desperately to pass between the warp storms of the Maelstrom and the Planet of the Sorcerers, they are riven by strands of astral fire woven by the Cult of Magic.

### 6. Cult of Knowledge – Remnant of the Dark Age

Scores of sects from the Cult of Knowledge repeatedly besiege and withdraw from the forge world Incaladion. In the carnage, one of the hallowed STCs held on the planet disappears.

### 7. Cult of Change – Unspoilt Flesh

In a gruelling campaign against the Sons of the Phoenix Chapter of Primaris Space Marines, the Thousand Sons take many of their enemies as live captives for their arcane experiments.

### 8. Cult of Duplicity – Web of Heresy

On worlds across the Imperium, Chaos Cultists arise and swear allegiance to the Cult of Duplicity. All claim that they are the warriors chosen by Tzeentch to bring ruin to the galaxy.

### 9. Cult of Manipulation – Burnt Offerings

Scores of worlds have been immolated in great sacrificial rituals before the coming of Hive Fleet Kronos, though whether these are designed to repel or lure the Tyranids is uncertain.

# THE PRISM OF WARFARE

**When the Thousand Sons march to war, the very stars tremble before their displays of sorcerous might, great swathes of the galaxy are consumed by warpfire, and anarchy and madness reign supreme. Yet each battle is but a component in their impenetrable stratagems, a single rite with a purpose inscrutable to all but the most twisted of minds.**

Though the Thousand Sons perpetrate their horrific wars throughout the galaxy, they do not see warfare as an end unto itself. Instead, through their studied violence they seek to wreak change upon the galaxy and to draw to themselves power and knowledge. By divining the currents of fate – both past and future – they identify crux points in time, moments where calamitous upheaval can be wrought for the glory of Tzeentch.

To aid in their grand designs, the Thousand Sons launch myriad raids on the worlds of the Imperium and xenos planets alike. Amidst the fires of these incursions they wrest arcane technologies from long-forgotten reliquaries, despoil temples of their sacred tomes and bend the faith of the masses to Tzeentch's ever-shifting purposes. The lore of millennia is consumed and digested by the rapacious minds of the Legion's Sorcerers, who glean from it hidden truths that help guide them along their ruinous path.

In their campaigns the Thousand Sons conquer vast tracts of realspace from which they draw the resources for their arcane war efforts. As they advance across the stars, their knowledge-lust brings them to sites of eldritch power, places saturated with the magic of profane rituals performed millennia ago. Some are worlds whose ancient inhabitants worshipped the Chaos Gods; others are planets with hateful entities buried deep beneath their surface. The baleful energy that hangs thick around such sites creates weak points in the veil separating realspace from the warp. Here, the Thousand Sons commune with empyric consciousnesses, beckoning them to enter the material plane and entreating them to share prescient visions of the skeins of fate.

These places of power also serve as anchor-points to which Exalted Sorcerers and Daemon Princes tether their enormous, system-spanning spells. Gigantic hexes are etched into the fabric of space itself, corrupting the reality that lies within their

bounds and causing it to tear violently open. From these gaping wounds the warp bleeds into existence, ravaging the minds of mortals with nightmarish perplexions and birthing daemonic beasts that descend hungrily upon the worlds of the living.

The sects of the Thousand Sons prosecute their wars in various ways and towards various ends. Some blaze like a comet as they carve their ruinous warpath through space. The psychic scream preceding their onslaught is a portent of doom, heralding to all before them the horrors that will soon be brought into being. Others conduct their campaigns in more subtle ways, silently preparing their offensives until the moment to strike is at hand. The thrallbands of these sects insinuate themselves throughout a war zone, whereupon they work to sever those strands of fate that would oppose their total victory. Psychic whispers are sent echoing through the immaterium to misdirect their enemies, time and space are bent to steer battlefleets wildly off course,

and the currents of the warp are shifted so that enemy psykers are consumed by the horrendous backfire of their arcane machinations. Such malefic dissimulation can even allow the Sorcerers of a thrallband to enter the mind of an enemy general, reaping from them battle plans or erasing carefully considered countermeasures from their memories. As combat commences the general's army faces impossibly superior intelligence, and the Thousand Sons slaughter their floundering opponents with brutal precision.

For thousands of years the Sons of Magnus have been a scourge upon the galaxy, and over that time many amongst their ranks have fallen in battle. But the Rubric of Ahriman – whilst stripping the Legion's warriors of their corporeality – rendered those it touched immortal. The dust containing the remnant essence of these warriors has been poured out on countless battlefields, blown from rents blasted in their arcanely sealed armour and trampled into the mud. When drawn together by

a Sorcerer, the warrior's essence can be rejoined with its armour and the spectral soldier can rise once more. Sorcerers seeking to raise an army of Rubricae hunt out the remains of the fallen, burning to the ground cities that have been built atop forgotten sites of battle. Any surviving inhabitants are swiftly massacred by the newly risen warriors.

Ambitious Sorcerers also go to great lengths to procure Daemon Engines with which they can loose even greater destruction upon their enemies. Fell pacts are made with Warpsmiths and the devotees of the Dark Mechanicum who forge abominations of metal infused with empyric entities – the Thousand Sons offering sorcerous knowledge in exchange for the creation of these daemonic machines. Such pacts are fraught with treachery, for both the Thousand Sons and the Chaos smiths seek only to further their own standing with the Ruinous Powers, and will gladly betray one another when they can find an opportunity.

There are some in the galaxy for whom the Thousand Sons' hatred burns more brightly than others – the Space Wolves who sundered their home world, the Death Guard who worship the Rot Lord Nurgle – but all who bar the paths laid out

by Tzeentch feel the piercing gaze of the Thousand Sons bear down upon them. Of late, the Aeldari known as the Harlequins have been subjected to this focused fury, for these guardians of the webway seek to protect their labyrinth dimension from the passage of Magnus' Legion.

A sect of the Thousand Sons may join forces with the warbands of another Chaos Legion, only to turn upon their allies when the fickle winds of fate shift, or they may drive xenos invaders from an Imperial world only to sacrifice the planet's population in a pyric ritual. Individual sects within the Thousand Sons may even go to war with one another as the cryptic machinations of the Great Conspirator set kin against kin. In this seeming madness lies the method of Tzeentch. Through continual anarchy and upheaval his will is made manifest throughout the galaxy, and upon his favoured mortal champions he bestows his manifold gifts.

Ultimately, each Sorcerer in the Thousand Sons is driven by selfish desire. Their thirst for arcane power is insatiable, leading them inexorably down the path that leads towards daemonhood. Only those most faithful to their patron god receive this blessing, and in their wake they leave centuries of anguish and destruction.

# ANNALS OF THE ARCANE

For ten millennia, the Thousand Sons have fought in the Long War against the Imperium, winding the strands of fate to their own malign purposes. Armies, civilizations and countless worlds have burnt in their blasphemous wars, and from the ashes of these conflagrations ever greater horrors have been brought into being.

## M31 THE GREAT CHANGE

### The Burning of Prospero

Leman Russ and his Space Wolves, along with contingents of the Legio Custodes and the Sisters of Silence, arrive on the Thousand Sons' home world to carry out the execution of Magnus' Legion. The savagery they unleash leaves the planet in flames and the Thousand Sons fighting for their very existence. Though Magnus is felled by the Wolf King, he is able to cast a spell to spirit himself and his sons away, saving their lives but damning them for eternity by pledging his allegiance to Tzeentch. The names of those who despoiled Prospero are never forgotten by the Thousand Sons.

### The Horus Heresy

The Thousand Sons join Horus and the other Chaos Legions as they strive to annihilate the Imperium. Though they fail to reduce Terra to cinders, the Sons of Magnus delve deep into the Emperor's Palace, learning many of his hidden secrets before retreating to the Eye of Terror.

### The Rubric of Ahriman

Ahriman and his cabal weave a great spell in an attempt to rid the Legion of their harrowing mutations. When unleashed, this Rubric reduces the vast majority of the Thousand Sons to dust, and entombs what remains of their spirits within warp-infused armour. Discovering what his most trusted son has wrought upon the Legion, Magnus becomes enraged, but Tzeentch intervenes and Magnus spares Ahriman's life, instead casting him out as an exile.

## M32-M41 AGE OF SECRECY

### Siege of the Fang

Magnus' vengeful gaze falls upon Fenris, and through a series of false visions he lures the Great Companies of the Space Wolves away from their lair. His assault on Fenris itself is devastating, but is at last repelled by warriors led by Bjorn the Fell-Handed.

### The Athenaeum of Kallimakus

Ahriman travels to Apollonia, where the works of Kallimakus the Remembrancer are guarded by a fanatical sect of warrior priests. These tomes are held in a grand citadel known as the Athenaeum, and contain records of the Thousand Sons Legion from the time of the Great Crusade. After a month-long siege, the defenders lie broken before Ahriman's forces. The Arch-Sorcerer plunders the writings from their vault before burning the library to ashes, intending that only he should hold the secrets contained within their pages.

### Omen of Omniscience

Hasophet, Magister of the Mind-Eaters thrallband, receives a vision of his Tzeentch-ordained destiny. He sees a time in his future when he will devour the thoughts and memories of an entire world, and in doing so will achieve apotheosis. The Mind-Eaters embark on the first of nine hundred and ninety-nine rites that will lead to this portended moment.

### The Feral War

Whilst mining the feral world of Aggaros, the Adeptus Mechanicus engage in what at first seems like an embarrassingly one-sided battle – that is until the primitives bring their flame-tongued shamans into the fray. The armies of the Adeptus Mechanicus find themselves burnt from the inside or crushed flat by invisible forces. The retreating Tech-Priests call in an old debt from the Relictors in order to renew the attack. Four days later, the Relictors' 3rd Company fights its way through psychic pyrotechnics of bewildering force to reach the hidden city of primitive tribes. Lining every road are dust-caked statues of the Thousand Sons facing a colossal effigy of Ahriman atop a pyramid of obsidian. When it is toppled, every one of the Thousand Sons comes to life, shrugging off the dust of centuries and opening fire on the Relictors with a hail of bolts. Not one of the Adeptus Mechanicus, nor their Relictor allies, survives.

### First War in the Webway

A coven of Sorcerers from the Kindled Spirits thrallband conducts a great ritual in the webway, hoping to gain access to the scream-filled city of Commorragh, the home of the Drukhari. Before their ritual is complete, hundreds of Drukhari, led by troupes of Harlequins, pour from an invisible portal and launch themselves at the Rubricae defending the coven. With their spell sundered, the Kindled Spirits counter-attack, their blasts of warpflame eventually breaching the fabric of the webway itself. As the arterial walls of the webway buckle and collapse outwards, the backlash strands the combatants in a shattered pocket-reality with no way out. There are whispers that the fighting has continued ever since, and that each warrior is fated to die and be reborn in an endless cycle for the rest of time.

## M41 AGE OF UNVEILING

### The Sacking of the Etiamnun Reclusiam

Mordant Hex, Sorcerer Lord of the Six-Cursed, is sent by Ahriman to the barren, airless planet of Etiamnun III on the distant Eastern Fringe. The arrival of Thousand Sons drop-ships shatters the peace that had shrouded the world for millennia, though the small community of hermits gathered within the central monastery meets the arrival with quiet, contemplative acceptance. Hex's forces advance steadily through the mountain passes, directly towards the gates of the hermitage where he strikes the giant adamantium doors nine times. As the doors yawn open, many of those inside are wrenched into the cold vacuum of the planet's surface, while those who remain in sealed chambers are swiftly hunted down and massacred. Even facing death at the hands of the Six-Cursed, the inhabitants give little or no resistance. When all are dead, Hex descends into the heart of the mountain complex, to a long-forgotten chamber buried under layers of ancient Imperial construction. Within the chamber is the prize for which Hex was sent – an entrance to the webway.

### Fortress of Infinities

The Imperial Fists strike force Anvil of Dorn boards a fire-wreathed space hulk on the western fringe of the Segmentum Solar. Within, they encounter Manat, Exalted Sorcerer of the Cult of Time, and after a gruelling war of attrition through mutating corridors, Captain Dantarian strikes down the Thousand Sons warlord in single combat. But in the moment of the Exalted Sorcerer's death there is a crack of aetheric power, and the Imperial

Fists find themselves back on their strike cruiser, preparing to board the space hulk as though for the first time. Only an unquiet flicker buried deep within each battle-brother's psyche suggests they may have walked this path before, and none can determine why they seem to have sustained so many casualties before even engaging the enemy. They battle Manat again, and again the Exalted Sorcerer's death transports them to the moment before the siege. After eight iterations the Anvil of Dorn is all but obliterated, and the ninth sees Captain Dantarian alone march aboard the space hulk, there to meet his death against the laughing Manat.

### Threading the Labyrinth
After years of gruesome crusades within the webway, Ahriman approaches the location of the Black Library, a vast and ancient repository of Aeldari knowledge. The Arch-Sorcerer bypasses the sanctum's Harlequin defenders and spectral guardians by projecting himself inside the Black Library's halls, allowing his physical body to transcribe onto hermetic parchment what his astral self sees. In doing so, he is able to create a copy of the fabled *Tome Labyrinthus*, the map to the hidden passages of the webway.

### Crystallised Night
An endless psychic scream lures Vasellisk the Shrouded, Sorcerer warlord of the Night Lords, to the obsidian mines on Xanthematos. As his warband sets about butchering the Imperial work crews, the terror of those slain continues to linger in the form of disembodied warp-gheists. The sight of spectral figures crowding the mines and howling with fear blinds Vasellisk to the true sorcery at play, for the planet has been hex-bound by Hasophet and his Mind-Eaters. As Vasellisk revels in the resonant terror, the Mind-Eaters seal the mines with the Night Lords inside. In the final twist of Hasophet's curse, the spirits of the dead burst into warpfire, filling the subterranean tunnels with screaming flame. By the time the mines are reopened, every last Night Lord has been reduced to ash – all except for Vasellisk the Shrouded, whose body has been melted into a lump of dark glass. This Shrouded Crystal is the foreseen prize of Hasophet's seven hundred and sixty-fifth rite, and it pulses with the psychic energy of the Sorcerer it once was.

### Destinies Entwined
To enact a plan that will transform the galaxy forever, Magnus the Red summons his exiled son – Ahzek Ahriman – back

to the Planet of the Sorcerers. There he entreats the Arch-Sorcerer to once more work with him towards a common goal.

### A Curse Returns
Shortly after reuniting with their long-lost Wulfen brethren, the Space Wolves find their home system engulfed by raging warp storms and a massive daemonic invasion. The Grey Knights and Dark Angels arrive to aid the Sons of Russ in expelling the threat, but the Imperial forces are coerced into a state of infighting by one of Tzeentch's most devious Daemon servants – the Changeling. It is the Grey Knights who first notice the warp storms forming a pattern, one recorded in their oldest tomes of lore and not seen in the galaxy for ten thousand years. It is a symbol of vengeance last used on Prospero by the Thousand Sons.

### A World for a World
As the home system of the Space Wolves is being overrun by Daemons, nine Silver Towers appear in the skies above Fenris. From their warped halls pour ranks of Thousand Sons, ready to wreak vengeance on the Chapter that destroyed their home world. Swarms of braying Tzaangors and mutated Cultists charge across the frozen plains, with Rubric Marines and Scarab Occult Terminators marching close behind. From hidden portals more Thousand Sons emerge onto the Fenrisian steeps, exiles brought back into the fold by Ahriman. By following the Arch-Sorcerer through the webway they are able to take the Space Wolves and their allies by surprise, incinerating the Adeptus Astartes with crackling psychic energy as they burst from the labyrinthine dimension.

As the Imperial lines hold out against the onslaught, the Silver Towers align with sites of geomantic power and begin siphoning the internal energy of Fenris, and on the third day the air is riven with fire. Sorcerers around the planet pour their psychic energy into this sky-fire, and within each of the Silver Towers a captive Space Wolf is boiled alive in a cauldron of gore. The

conflux of dark magics creates a weak point in reality – a doorway through which strides the Daemon Primarch Magnus. The Crimson King joins with Ahriman and his other most powerful acolytes, and together they begin their rituals in the hearts of the Silver Towers. The resultant flow of mutagenic energy ravages the surface of Fenris, causing the molten magma powering the Fang to fill with Daemons and bubble up to the surface.

It is only when the neighbouring planet of Midgardia is destroyed that the Silver Towers disappear from the system, but any Imperial celebration is premature – unbeknownst to the Space Wolves, the psychic harvest reaped by the towers from Midgardia's demise has given Magnus the power he needs to enact a plan of unimaginable scope.

### The Blood-filled Gullet
With the Fang's defences disabled, the Thousand Sons march towards the Space Wolves citadel. But it is in the Wolf's Gullet canyon that the defenders of Fenris make their stand. Magnus himself towers above the fire and the fury, shredding tanks, attack craft and squads of Space Marines with bolts of coruscating warp energy. Hoping to fell the Daemon Primarch, Egil Iron Wolf fires a lascannon blast at Magnus' cyclopean eye, but with a thought the Crimson King freezes the bolt in mid-air before translocating Egil in front of his own shot and allowing the las-beam to incinerate its firer. This momentary distraction gives the Great Wolf Logan Grimnar the opening he needs to cleave the Axe Morkai through Magnus' armour, breaking the protective wards formed by the Blue Scribes of Tzeentch. As Magnus howls in pain, a gleaming throng of Grey Knight Purifiers begin to incant the rites of banishment. The white flames pouring from their blades envelop Magnus, and in a flare of light brighter than the Fenrisian sun, the Crimson King, the Thousand Sons and their daemonic hordes are banished back to the warp. The defenders of Fenris believe they have halted whatever dark plan Magnus had, but far across the stars there is a rumbling in the void…

### Magic Made Manifest
Powered by the death of Midgardia and its inhabitants, the Planet of the Sorcerers bursts violently from the warp into realspace, coming to rest in sight of the burnt husk of Prospero. Sitting atop his throne, Magnus gazes outwards at a galaxy irrevocably changed.

### Dark Confluence

Abaddon the Despoiler unites the fractious Traitor Legions in preparation for his Thirteenth Black Crusade. Magnus the Red refuses Abaddon's call to war, but Ahriman sees potential in the scale of the Despoiler's plans. The Arch-Sorcerer sends several thrallbands towards the ice moon of Klaisius in the Cadia System, ostensibly in aid of the Despoiler's building crusade. However, their movements are a distraction designed to cover Ahriman's true motivations, for he foresees that this moon will soon become a nexus of fate in the schemes of Tzeentch.

### Wages of Change

After undermining the millennium-long battle plan of Korthuphos – an Exalted Sorcerer of the Cult of Magic – Hasophet is challenged to a psychic duel. As the two lock minds in combat it is clear that Korthuphos is the more powerful psyker, but Hasophet unsheathes the Dagger of Reflections, acquired centuries ago during his eighty-seventh rite. The mind-flames cast out by Korthuphos are drawn towards the shimmering dagger before being forced back in a thunderous wave, pulverising the brain matter of the Exalted Sorcerer. Korthuphos begins to slump over with liquid oozing from his helm, but before he hits the ground Hasophet plunges the ensorcelled dagger into his fallen opponent's chest, carving out his still-beating hearts. They are the trophies of his eight hundred and twenty-eighth rite.

### Second War in the Webway

Hidden daemonic spies seeded throughout the webway draw Ahriman's eye to the Reborn of the Ynnari, for in their resurrection he sees hope for his own fallen Legion. In the wake of Cadia's fall during the Thirteenth Black Crusade, the Arch-Sorcerer leads a contingent of Thousand Sons into the webway, there to lay an ambush for the unsuspecting Aeldari forces that are rushing towards Klaisius. Just as the Ynnari are entering the Psychedelta, Ahriman sacrifices nine hundred and ninety-nine captives to Tzeentch to complete his ritual of translocation, shifting him, his warriors and his Daemon thralls to the Ynnari's location. Warpfire, ensorcelled bolts and the flicker of monomolecular blades fill the fractal tunnels as the armies clash. In the midst of the carnage, Ahriman creates a void-like pocket reality outside the walls of the webway, and into this emptiness he transports the champions of the enemy, the Triumvirate of Ynnead.

As Ahriman prepares to wrench the knowledge he seeks from his dying captives, Yvraine – the Ynnari emissary of the recently awakened God of the Dead – demonstrates the power she can offer by restoring to life a dozen Rubric Marines. The resurrected Thousand Sons are staggered by their sudden awakening, knowing not where they are or who they fight, yet they recognise their battle-brother Ahzek Ahriman whom they have not beheld with living eyes for ten millennia. Filled with a mixture of elation and grief at seeing his warriors restored, Ahriman yanks Ynnead's luminaries back inside the webway before they perish. No sooner than the Triumvirate are safe, a Wraithknight slices through the superstructure of the tunnel, creating a yawning chasm between the Aeldari and the Thousand Sons. The Yncarne – Avatar of Ynnead – inhales mightily as the Aeldari forces withdraw, pulling the reanimated Thousand Sons over the precipice into the void. Ahriman screams in horror as these flesh and blood warriors tumble away. They are lost to him once more, but he now knows that the reversal of his Rubric is possible, and he knows who has the power to do it.

### An Ancient Foe Awakens

Word reaches Magnus of the resurrection of Roboute Guilliman. Knowing the loyalist warlord will try to reunite with the Emperor on Terra, Magnus reads the fluctuating strands of fate to divine his brother's path. He leads his armada to the edge of the raging nether-realm of warp storms known as the Maelstrom, and there waits for the arrival of the Terran Crusade. When Guilliman's fleet emerges from its warp-jump, it is greeted with pummelling fire from the heretic craft. Against overwhelming numbers and the element of surprise, Guilliman is still somehow able to direct the Imperial ships to hold out. But the Crimson King calls to the warp, summoning coiling tendrils of power to coalesce around the ships of the Terran Crusade, drawing them into the Maelstrom. Magnus knows this is not the hour of the loyalist Primarch's death, but Guilliman's fate has been set on a path most suited to the Crimson King's designs.

### Gods of War

Magnus waits for Roboute Guilliman to make his way to Terra, but instead of travelling to the portal beneath the Emperor's Palace, as Magnus had hoped, the Terran Crusade emerges on Luna. Nevertheless, Magnus follows the beleaguered Imperial force, storming from the webway onto the moon's surface to stand beneath the orb of Holy Terra. As Magnus and Guilliman behold each other, the Crimson King smiles in anticipation of the combat to come. His Rubric Marines and Scarab Occult Terminators advance upon the Imperial forces, spraying them with gouts of warpfire and fusillades of inferno bolts. Magnus' psychic might erupts in a destructive nova, shattering the bodies of his enemies and shielding his own forces from harm. Guilliman then launches himself at Magnus, and the moon's crust trembles with the impact of their blows. Across the plains, craters and wreckage of ancient frigates the two demigods battle, Guilliman a titan of martial prowess, Magnus armed with the unbridled sorceries of the warp.

As the Primarchs fight, the ranks of Thousand Sons continue to pour unending fire into the remnants of the Terran Crusade and their Imperial reinforcements. Guilliman's ally – the Shadowseer Sylandri Veilwalker – weaves her own magic to undo the runic bindings placed by the Sorcerers of the Thousand Sons on the webway portal. With a roar of hate and rage Guilliman strikes his opponent, while Magnus unleashes an uncontrolled sorcerous blast. The resulting shock wave sends the Crimson King reeling back through the portal, and in a fateful instant Veilwalker seals the gateway behind him. Within the labyrinth-dimension Magnus roars in fury. The day he saw fated to visit ruin on the Emperor has been taken from him. But his anger is short-lived, for looking to the future he sees a great darkness that will soon envelop the Imperium, and many paths of fate that will lead him to the vengeance he seeks…

### The Galaxy Ruptures

The baleful energies emanating from the Planet of the Sorcerers intermingle with that of countless gathering warp storms, rending the galaxy across its length. The massive outpouring of mutative power destroys entire systems and briefly extinguishes the Astronomican – the Emperor's guiding light that unites the Imperium. Laughter and gleeful snarls echo deep within the Chaos dimension.

# M41 AGE OF BURNING

## Broken Shield

The Cult of Manipulation forge a hex to extinguish the Aspis star in Segmentum Solar. The growing solar storm alerts the Adeptus Custodes to the Thousand Sons' machinations, and a squad of Allarus Custodians, joined by a Grey Knights strike force and a large contingent of Skitarii, set out to locate and eradicate the cabal, but as they approach the Aspis System an enormous solar flare separates the Imperial forces. While the Grey Knights and Skitarii find and destroy the profane wards sustaining the hex, the Adeptus Custodes are sent adrift through the warp, into the clutches of the waiting Thousand Sons.

## The Stygius Kingdom

Magnus the Red leads a devastating assault on the Stygius Sector. Cut off from the Astronomican, the Imperial defenders fall quickly to Cultist uprisings, daemonic invasions and attacks from scores of thrallbands. Only the stubbornness of the Mordian Iron Guard and the arrival of the Aeldari prevent the system from being overrun, though even these events have long been foreseen by Magnus, and are part of his wider plan for the transformation of Stygius.

## The Beast Within

On the high-grav world of Krachordia, the abhuman Ogryn tribes hunt down a mutant beast that has been roaming the stalagmite jungle. As they hack the writhing creature apart, they find an undulating sac lodged within its innards. The hunters feel a strange inclination to recover this mysterious growth, and so bring it to the tribal elders who deem it 'good' and place it in the centre of their settlement. Over time the sac begins to shed light of multiple hues. Eventually it splits open and from within emerges a creature radiant and beautiful to the eyes of the tribesmen. To them it resembles a perfectly formed human, and they weep in the presence of its magnificence. As they fall to their knees in worship their own bodies begin to change, becoming more like the being they adore. Months later, the Astra Militarum fleets arrive to collect their tithe of warriors from Krachordia. They find no trace of the Ogryn tribes – only a world overrun with hulking Chaos Spawn.

## The Impassable Sea

Space Wolves from Engir Krakendoom's Great Company set a course for Prospero, hoping to reach the Planet of the Sorcerers and once more bring ruin to the Thousand Sons' home world. But no matter what path they take, eerily sentient warp eddies fling them far off track.

## The Silent War

A cloud of particulate dust falls over the heavily fortified spire-convent of the Sisters of Silence on Gassima. It is soon followed by a more destructive storm as suits of Rubric armour bearing the sigil of the Blades of Magnus fall from the sky like meteors, smashing through vaulted ceilings and cratering the courtyards. As the Sisters of Silence reel from the bombardment, sheets of lightning crack through the atmosphere and the dust cloud coalesces around the lifeless Rubric suits. The dust – which is in fact the essence of Thousand Sons warriors – pours into the armour, and one by one they stand up and raise their weapons. The spire-convent is obliterated in the battle, and every Sister of Silence slaughtered, though even faced with death not one allows herself to scream.

## Power Unbound

In their war with the Necrons of the Nephrekh Dynasty, the Silver Sons loose a quartet of Heldrakes upon a Tesseract Vault. The winged monstrosities tear the prison open, freeing the C'tan Shard within and allowing it to begin a years-long rampage through Nephrekh space.

## The Psychophage of Mangel III

Hasophet and his Mind-Eaters descend upon the Imperial hive world of Mangel III amidst an ongoing T'au invasion. Before landing the Sorcerer shatters the Shrouded Crystal in orbit, casting its shards throughout the atmosphere to summon an impenetrable darkness which surrounds the planet. Cut off from orbital reinforcements and relays, the T'au armies and planetary defence forces continue fighting in utter confusion. In the Valley of Sacrifice, between the lines of the battling armies, the Mind-Eaters array the trophies and fetishes acquired from their nine hundred and ninety-eight preceding rites in a great crescent, and between the horns of the crescent Hasophet mounts an enormous pyre. From its pinnacle he beholds the encroaching T'au and Imperial forces – they are to be his, their thoughts and memories devoured as was foretold.

Holding aloft the hearts of Korthuphos, Hasophet ignites his pyre with their blood, incanting an oath to Tzeentch as the flames begin to lap his armour. The sudden rush of energy towards Hasophet shreds the minds of the hundreds of thousands of combatants on Mangel III, siphoning their very life force into the Sorcerer. But as the Grand Conspirator's changes take hold Hasophet screams in agony. The armies on the horizon are pulled physically towards him like gnats caught in a thundering vortex. Ranks of screaming bodies and enormous war engines fly across the darkened land, colliding with Hasophet where they are quickly absorbed by his warping form. His body devours metal and flesh with equal voraciousness as it continues to grow, howling in excruciation from newly forming maws. His mass pupates, not into the form of a Daemon Prince, but to that of a Mutalith Vortex Beast. The warp vortex emanating from the hideous creature extends outwards with each newly consumed sacrifice until it encircles the planet, and with a final mind-tearing scream Mangel III itself is torn from realspace. In its place there is left only a perpetual dark shroud and an echo of Hasophet's final, pitiful cry.

## The Subsumation of the Exiles

A dozen exiled sects are summoned by the Rehati to the Planet of the Sorcerers. Through psychic communication and blazing runes cast throughout the stars, the Rehati inform the leader of each sect that they have two options – either consolidate their forces with the bulk of the Thousand Sons, or suffer the full wrath of their Primarch for refusing his clemency. Of those summoned, eleven arrive at the Planet of the Sorcerers. The returning armies are arrayed in the mustering grounds of Tizca wherein the Rehati begin the rites of reunification. As the final act of subservience, every living Sorcerer amongst the exiles is summoned to the Altar of Fates where nine drops of their blood are drawn and cast into the ever-burning fires. At this moment, the massed ranks of Rubric Marines and Scarab Occult Terminators from the eleven sects turn to the Rehati, kneeling down before their new rulers in perfect unison. Rising, they simultaneously turn towards the Sorcerers huddled on the Altar of Fate, raise their weapons and unleash devastasting payloads against their masters of old.

## The Road to Resurrection

Having witnessed the ability of Yvraine to restore the Thousand Sons afflicted by the Rubric, Ahriman begins gathering his forces. After ten thousand years he knows where to find the knowledge he has been seeking, and so he trains his prescient vision on the Drukhari city of Commorragh.

Though at times the manifold sects of the Thousand Sons seem divided, or even opposed to one another, this is merely an illusion – a result of the incomprehensibility of Magnus' ambitions and the unfathomable will of Tzeentch. Every thrallband and each Sorcerer has a role to play, and they are all guided towards the fate envisioned by their Daemon Primarch.

# MAGNUS THE RED

## THE CRIMSON KING, DAEMON PRIMARCH OF TZEENTCH

Magnus was created by the Emperor of Man as a giant, physically and mentally towering over his fellow Primarchs. His abilities as a psyker were unsurpassed by all save the Emperor himself, and with honour and cunning he led the Thousand Sons to countless victories in the Great Crusade. During this time he fed his insatiable hunger for knowledge, harvesting the sorcerous learnings of the human cults and xenos races he eradicated. This dark path led to Magnus' judgement at the Council of Nikaea, the burning of his home world at the hands of the Space Wolves, and his ultimate covenant with the God of Sorcery, Tzeentch.

Where once Magnus stood as a paragon of Humanity, he is now a monstrous creature of Chaos, a Daemon Primarch bound to the sinister and subtle will of the Great Conspirator. His skin, ever red, crackles and glows with the warp-matter it has absorbed, and from his back sprout enormous wings emblazoned with runes of Tzeentchian power. With his single eye he sees through the immaterium and realspace alike, weaving the strands of manifold futures and winding them to form a noose with which he can ensnare his enemies. Though he once sought knowledge for its own purpose, he now seeks only that which will ensure the Imperium burns.

In a galaxy riven by war, there are few things more terrifying to behold on the battlefield than a Daemon Primarch. Where Magnus strides, the fabric of reality strains and breaks, time and space wrenching violently apart to allow his passage. The very sight of him sears the mind with shifting, paradoxical images, glimpses of the warp incomprehensible to mortal thought. Those over whom his shadow falls are plunged into darkness, their egos collapsed into a dense singularity as Magnus' daemonic presence encroaches upon their psyches. Even dauntless warriors who have braved countless horrific conflicts find their courage torn to shreds when the lord of the Thousand Sons is stoked to fury.

From the glowing fires of Magnus' eye come blasts of raw psychic energy. With each earth-shattering bolt Titans and armoured columns are torn from reality, their very substance reduced to clouds of screaming atoms. As the Daemon Primarch draws near to his foes they are caught in a field of fluctuating energy, an aura of malefic sentience that twists existence to suit Magnus' will. The most impenetrable defences are laid bare by this warping influence, leaving the enemy open to slaughter.

In his taloned hands Magnus bears a flame-wreathed blade that takes whatever murderous form its wielder conceives. With this he carves through the enemy's ranks, bisecting tank hulls and torsos, severing souls from their corporeal bodies. For those not instantly reduced to a pool of gore or puff of flame an even worse fate awaits – the ensorcelled staff mutates the riven flesh of its victims, infusing them with empyric power to birth writhing Chaos Spawn.

The plate armour covering Magnus' daemonic body is embellished with Tzeentchian runes, their profane symbology creating a tapestry of madness. A great horned crown adorns the Crimson King's head, through which he exudes an aura of protective energy around himself, shielding his physical and mental essence. The futility of defying Magnus' wrath becomes clear when enemy fire

dissipates harmlessly before striking him; psychic bolts fizzle into innocuous sparks and gargantuan chainblades grind to a halt against this aetheric barrier.

Magnus directs entire cults of Thousand Sons warriors in battle. With these armies he shares a small fraction of his indomitable might, giving to the soulless Rubricae and Scarab Occult Terminators a portion of violent vitality, and bolstering the already ravenous ambitions of the still-living Sorcerers. They are his greatest weapon, guided by coercion and fate to do his fell bidding, and through them he visits his wrath upon the galaxy.

---

## THE BOOK OF MAGNUS

Towards the end of the Great Crusade, Magnus collected the lore and knowledge he had uncovered in a single arcane tome. Ever sensitive to the presence of psychic power, Magnus drew alike upon the forbidden knowledge of the mystics and soothsayers of destroyed human cults and the eldritch remnants of xenos ruins on planets scoured for Imperial reclamation. Through his masterwork, Magnus made a record of psychic powers unknown to the Primarchs and Librarians of other Space Marine Legions, some of which he would impart to the Sorcerers of his Legion.

Since the Thousand Sons' fall, the Book of Magnus has become unbound by physical laws – the words written on its pages crawl and shift as though alive, changing constantly in shape and size. Amongst the few Imperial scholars who are aware of the tome's existence, some believe it expands to accommodate the ever-widening knowledge of its creator. Others hold that the book gained a wholly separate sentience when Magnus pledged himself to Tzeentch, and that its perpetual mutations are born of its subservience to the Changer of the Ways. In either case, to look upon its pages is to invite madness into the mortal mind.

The Book of Magnus has manifested several times throughout the ages. What is believed to be the original copy rests in the innermost chamber atop the Tower of the Cyclops, and is borne by Magnus when he strides to war. Ahriman also possesses a copy which he took with him when he was exiled from the Planet of the Sorcerers. Of the other copies said to exist, the location of only one is known for sure. Held by the Aeldari deep within the webway, the screams of its sorcerous pages echo through the halls of the Black Library.

# EXALTED SORCERERS

Amongst the manifold warp-wielders of the Thousand Sons there are those whose skill, cunning and naked ambition burn bright as a raging star. For these Sorcerers, the power that can be achieved within the Legion is bound only by the limits of their own sanity, and they delve ever further into the most forbidden psychic disciplines to perfect their ruinous spellcraft. Those whose souls are not torn to shreds by the empyric forces they encounter may rise to the rank of Exalted. The members of this echelon are the most favoured of Tzeentch's mortal servants, powerful warlords who command the Legion's armies and who steer the course of the galaxy towards one of the horrific fates they have foreseen.

Without fail, Exalted Sorcerers are exceptional warriors. Their genetically augmented bodies were built for the savagery of combat and through the gifts of their patron god have been enhanced by mutation – some have grown additional limbs or have eyes that exude flames when they look hatefully upon their foes. By drawing upon their reserves of psychic energy, an Exalted Sorcerer can further bolster his martial prowess in terrifying ways. Complex spells are woven amidst the swirl of combat that allow them to perceive the movements of their enemies, seeing feints and ambushes in their mind's eye then striking back with deadly precision. With a sonorous curse they fire malefic bolts to blast their foes limb from limb or entangle them with cruel hexes.

An Exalted Sorcerer's rank in the Legion's hierarchy is not fixed – as servants of Tzeentch they are acutely aware that the favour given them may change at any moment. As such they must strive tirelessly to maintain their position, subjugating those who covet their power through manipulation, deceit and open displays of force. In this way Exalted Sorcerers gather beneath them many thralls – lesser Sorcerers who serve the wiles of their master. Many of these Sorcerers are unaware that they are pawns in an Exalted Sorcerer's grandiose schemes, for their enslavement is veiled by subtle lies and constantly shifting promises.

To an Exalted Sorcerer, the warriors they command are a resource to be deployed, akin to the sacrificial components used in one of his rituals. An Exalted Sorcerer seeks only his own selfish ends, and will send ranks of Rubricae and dozens of subordinate Sorcerers to die if this will further a much greater goal. However, they are not wasteful with the armies at their disposal, and carefully measure the ripple effect each thrallband's actions will have in the vast sea of causality. Each and every battle is but a small component of a war, and war itself is only a means through which they see change spread across the galaxy. An Exalted Sorcerer will pursue any strategy that his portents deem effective, and can change tactics with fluid ease as the shifting tides of battle give spark to his dark imagination. For most Exalted Sorcerers, the ultimate goal is to prove themselves worthy of Tzeentch's greatest blessing, to be freed of their mortal forms and transformed into a being of even greater power – a Daemon Prince.

## DISCS OF TZEENTCH

The Architect of Fate bestows many gifts upon his mortal servants. Amongst the most coveted of these are Discs of Tzeentch. Those who prove themselves useful to their patron god may be blessed with one of these daemonic steeds, allowing them to fly across the battlefield and rain psychic destruction down from on high. The Tzeentchian mount tethers itself to its master's psyche, entwining the thoughts of each into a single, symbiotic whole. Many Discs of Tzeentch are covered in undulating eyes or other sensory organs which feed directly into the mind of the rider, and all bear rows of jagged blades and serrated teeth with which to eviscerate their master's enemies. The methods by which Discs of Tzeentch achieve flight are varied and mutable. Some emit jets of warpflame from maws on their underside, whereas others simple surge forwards by bending the dimensions of realspace around them.

# AHRIMAN
## ARCH-SORCERER OF TZEENTCH

Ahzek Ahriman is the most powerful Sorcerer in the Thousand Sons' history, second only to Magnus in psychic ability. Before their fall to Chaos, he was the Legion's Chief Librarian and Magister Templi of the Corvidae, entrusted with sifting through the shifting strands of fate to divine the Legion's future. He was a mighty military leader, the keeper of the Book of Magnus, and – ultimately – it was by his Rubric that the Thousand Sons succumbed to irrevocable damnation.

For the ruin he brought upon the Thousand Sons, Ahriman was cast from the Planet of the Sorcerers, banished until he had completed the impossible task of understanding the true nature of Tzeentch. Since then he has wandered in exile, gathering ranks of Rubricae and Sekhmet warriors to his side, seeking out the galaxy's most powerful artefacts and its most arcane secrets, and carving a complex path of fiery devastation through the Imperium.

Of late, Ahriman's baleful attention has been focused upon the Aeldari, for he believes they possess the knowledge he needs to restore the Thousand Sons to their former glory. He witnessed the eldritch power of the xenos race first-hand when Yvraine, Emissary of Ynnead, returned a dozen Rubric Marines to life. Though Ahriman claims to pursue this knowledge as a way of undoing the grim fate that has befallen his Legion, his true intentions – as always – are entirely inscrutable.

Though the paths of Ahriman and Magnus have been at odds for ten millennia, they have intersected in recent years. Through his knowledge of the webway, Ahriman has aided Magnus in conducting multiple surprise attacks from that nether-dimension into realspace. However, the ultimate fate of these most malefic psykers is known only to Tzeentch himself.

### THE BLACK STAFF OF AHRIMAN

The Black Staff of Ahriman is a weapon capable of sundering reality. Created by the Arch-Sorcerer himself, each separate component is a relic of immense power acquired through horrific wars and quests of despoilment. Its bladed tip is a remnant of the desecrated Spear of Shadows, taken from the dying hands of Farseer Kalrimon. Its haft is made from the charred fragments of Ahriman's own hequa staff that burned on Prospero during the Space Wolves' invasion. These and other relics were bound together in a profane ritual that brought the Black Staff into being, sending pained screams echoing through the immaterium. Though imperceptible to mortal eyes, the staff appears to those with witch-sight as a blazing scar of darkness in the warp, a black absence towards which psychic energy is inextricably drawn before being blasted out by Ahriman's destructive will.

# SORCERERS

A Sorcerer strides to the battlefield wreathed in scintillating flames and clouds of crackling aetheric lightning. With a cruel gesture he bends the fabric of time and space to his will, crushing the bones of his enemies in enfolded pockets of reality or flensing the sanity from their minds with a blasphemous whisper. Each Sorcerer is nightmare given mortal form, capable of harnessing fear and anger to drive an opposing army to tear itself apart.

Sorcerers serve as leaders in the multitudinous thrallbands of the Thousand Sons. It is they who command the marching ranks of the Rubricae on the front lines and funnel screaming hordes of Cultists and Tzaangors towards the enemy. As the insanity surrounding the Sorcerer floods the battlefield, they intone rituals of summoning to draw Tzeentch's daemonic children through the veil between realspace and the immaterium. A Sorcerer often has free rein to prosecute psychic warfare as they see fit, but their actions are ultimately in service to their sect, and to a more powerful Exalted Sorcerer or Daemon Prince.

Despite their enthralment, Sorcerers are creatures of rampant ambition. As they serve their masters they also seek ways to undermine them, drawing power from secret cabals and forging treacherous pacts with empyric entities. As a Sorcerer grows in power, he risks succumbing to the weight of his own warp energy – many fall to uncontrolled mutation and become polymorphic Chaos Spawn. Yet their ambition drives them to take ever greater risks in the pursuit of power, for they hope one day to attain the rank of Exalted Sorcerer, and from there to become a blessed Daemon Prince of Tzeentch.

On occasion a powerful warp-mage from another Chaos Legion will be guided by Tzeentch to seek out the Planet of the Sorcerers and pledge his existence to Magnus. However, most of the Thousand Sons Sorcerers arise from the ranks of the Aspiring Sorcerers. These under-mages are often created from the psykers of Tzeentchian cults, who through profane demagoguery draw the attention of an invading sect. They are taken to Tizca, where they are subjected to ritual transformations to enhance their body and mind. Most are driven mad or are torn apart by the sudden influx of empyric energy; others die slow and agonizing deaths as warp-drenched augmentative organs mutate the host body. But those few who survive are born anew as witch-warriors of the Thousand Sons.

## FAMILIARS

The immaterium is home to innumerable malefic beings that readily lend their powers to those foolish enough to call upon them. To entreat such beings is perilous, and many who do so are devoured by the ravenous warp-creatures. Only a powerful Sorcerer can bend such an entity to his will, trapping its essence within an arcane object or host creature as a familiar. So bound, the familiar augments the Sorcerer's abilities, engorging him with raw psychic might. The practice of harnessing familiars – known as tutelaries – was a secret amongst the Thousand Sons before their fall to Chaos. Where other Imperial forces employed psybernetically enhanced creatures, the Sons of Magnus learnt through their studies of the power they could wield by calling upon the warp directly.

# DAEMON PRINCES OF TZEENTCH

For a Sorcerer of the Thousand Sons, the apotheosis of their service to the Grand Conspirator is to gain immortality as a Daemon Prince. The last fragment of their mortal soul – already warped by centuries of sadistic manipulation done unto others – is plunged into swirling darkness, never to return. Their flesh is riven with Chaos energy, their body growing to enormous proportions to accommodate a massive surge of raw empyric matter. Muscles bulge along elongated limbs, and hands twist into many-taloned claws that drip with magic. Much of their armour and weaponry is absorbed into their new form. The Tzeentchian runes and icons bedecking their wargear become embedded in sinew, where they pulsate with bestial vigour.

This metamorphosis renders the Daemon Prince completely unrecognisable from the living creature it once was. Its skin takes on colours more pleasing to the Changer of the Ways, growing intensely bright, terrifyingly dark, or taking on variegated hues in fluctuating configurations. Its very flesh shifts between translucency and absolute opaqueness, and curved horns and thorny gnarls sprout from the Daemon Prince's body. Some Daemon Princes grow great leathery wings with which they soar through the skies of battle; others develop a trailing cape of undulating tendrils. More esoteric changes may take form in a Daemon Prince as well – shadows that burn with darkest fire and warp all that they touch, or halos of light indescribable in colour that pierce the thin layer of sanity protecting a mortal's soul from the Daemon Prince's gaze.

Though their new-found power is immense, there are still other beings whom the Daemon Princes call master. Magnus the Red commands many Daemon Princes – they are his mightiest warlords, serving as members of his Rehati and leading his Legion's cults in conflagrant wars against the Imperium. The aura of raw magic emanating from a Daemon Prince invigorates those warriors who fight alongside him, giving them glimpses of the future and whispers of daemonic knowledge. A Daemon Prince's very existence is a manifestation of its Tzeentch-given power, and in its presence the will of the Architect of Fate is made manifest upon the battlefield. Plants wither and mutate into grotesque anomalies; the skin of enemy soldiers peels back to expose writhing muscle and shivering bone; adamantium vehicle plating and ferrocrete bunker walls erupt in gnashing mouths that cry out in anguish as the Daemon Prince approaches.

The weapons a Daemon Prince carries are well suited to their monstrous form. Where the Sorcerer may once have wielded an arcane staff or ensorcelled blade, a Daemon Prince sets about its slaughtering armed with a sword or axe wrought from warp-matter. Ripples of corruption are sent crashing outwards with each swing, and with such a weapon the Daemon Prince can sever the present from the past and future, ending an enemy champion's existence by erasing their very being. Others achieve their butchery with their talons, slicing through wave after wave of victims, spraying torrents of blood that ignite with warpfire. Those Daemon Princes in the Crimson King's service are masters of psychic malediction, and with a snarled word they can wrack an opposing army with hideous mutations or open a portal to the oblivion of the warp. Should a Daemon Prince somehow fall in battle, their existence persists in the immaterium, for they are tethered forever

to their patron god. By the will of Tzeentch, and by the power of their own undying hatred, they may return to the material plane to finish their fell works, and to hunt down those enemies who dared defy them.

Where other Tzeentchian entities can only exist outside the warp for short periods of time, evaporating from existence when the maelstrom of change-magic abates, Daemon Princes can sustain their corporeal forms by waging continuous campaigns of insanity and terror. Each fiery war prosecuted and every sacrificial ritual enacted is another pluck at the strings of fate. This feeds the Daemon Prince's essence, sustaining it in the material plane and filling it with fuel for its star-spanning sorceries.

# RUBRIC MARINES

Fearless, remorseless and utterly implacable, the Rubric Marines march to battle in gleaming ranks amidst clouds of eldritch energy. The eerie regularity of their footfalls is not a product of military drilling, but of the singular purpose to which all are bound. They are lifeless automata, the targets of the Rubric of Ahriman, whose mortal bodies have long since been reduced to dust. Whether the souls of these warriors were eradicated entirely, or whether some small fragment continues to linger, not even the most powerful mystics of the Thousand Sons can say. But when they are unleashed upon the Legion's enemies, the spark of battle-hunger returns and the Rubricae fight with ruinous proficiency.

The ancient Prosperine armour that houses their essence bears little resemblance to its former appearance, having been melded over many centuries by the empyric powers of the warp. Where once their raiments were the embodiment of Imperial might, they are now a testament to the will of Tzeentch. The articular servos and fibre bundles that give the interlocking ceramite plates movement are infused with sorcerous energy, providing the Rubric Marine with a semblance of animus. This same power coalesces around the armour, creating a protective shroud against incoming fire. Even those attacks that do manage to pierce the shell of a Rubric Marine have little effect, for they have no flesh to be torn by bolt or blade, and only by sundering the armour completely can they be taken down.

When a Rubric Marine does fall in battle, the desiccated remnants of their corporeal form pour from the rents in their armour and are scattered to the wind. As such, many worlds have ancient battlefields that are seeded with the dust of Rubric Marines. Yet even dispersed, the warrior is not granted the release of oblivion. Should the fragments of their armour be collected and resealed, the essence of the Rubric Marine can be returned to its vessel to once again serve the Thousand Sons. The sorceries required to achieve such a rebinding are as dangerous as they are powerful. A single misspoken syllable can kill the intoner or drive them insane. But should the profane rituals be successful, the essence dust of the Rubric Marine will be drawn back to its prison. Many Aspiring Sorcerers amongst the Legion will perform these rites, and the most skilled can will the essence of a Rubric Marine to coalesce even if the dust of its body has been strewn across an entire planet or buried deep beneath the surface.

Rubric Marines are forever yoked to those who have entrapped them. An Aspiring Sorcerer who has gained control over a squad of Rubric Marines can direct them in battle as a puppeteer would operate a marionette. Often, the Aspiring Sorcerer will use their enslaved soldiers as a bulwark against the enemy while they themselves work their dark magics. Should the Aspiring Sorcerer fall, the Rubric Marines continue to follow the path on which they have been set, killing and maiming until all before them have been obliterated.

Like their armour, the weapons borne by Rubric Marines are twisted mockeries of Imperial wargear. Their gun stocks are bedecked with ornate runes that writhe and mutate with shifting currents of empyric energy, and muzzles gape open and snap shut like the maws of unnatural creatures. The most common armament of the Rubric Marines is the inferno boltgun. The mass-reactive bolts they fire are charged with baleful sorcerous energies that are released upon impact, shredding the armour, flesh and soul of those they strike. The soulreaper cannon is a heavier and even more devastating weapon, and despite its great bulk a Rubric Marine can pour out a constant stream of fire without breaking their rhythmic stride. Some Rubric Marines march to battle armed with warpflamers. Though similar in appearance to the flamers used by other Chaos Legions, the warpflamer's gouts of fire burn through reality itself. Instead of simply incinerating that which they touch, the iridescent flames have a mutagenic effect. Matter engulfed by these flames is melted by searing heat before being fused back together in hideous configurations.

# SCARAB OCCULT TERMINATORS

Scarab Occult Terminators were once bodyguards to Magnus the Red. Like the others of their Legion, all but a handful were reduced to dust by the Rubric of Ahriman, and they now possess but a spectral shadow of their former intellect and ambition. However, as warriors they are more indomitable than ever. Their every action is geared towards the ruinous desires of those who control them, and what remains of their instinct is devoted solely to the destruction of their enemies.

Like the Rubric Marines, Scarab Occult Terminators fight at the behest of a sorcerous master. Some of these masters were part of the Scarab Occult at the time of Ahriman's mighty spell, and were robust enough of spirit and mind to resist its obliterative effects. Others are powerful mystics who have ascended the ranks of the Thousand Sons over many centuries and through twisted ingenuity earned a place amongst the vaunted Sekhmet. In either case, a Scarab Occult Sorcerer controls a nigh-unstoppable force of warrior-automata, capable of wading unharmed through masses of lesser enemy infantry.

The armour in which the warriors of the Scarab Occult are entombed is based upon pre-Heresy Terminator armour. Each suit was a relic of the Legion, but even before their fall to Tzeentch was complete the Thousand Sons had begun engraving their Terminator armour with profane inscriptions. This desecration continued after the Council of Nikaea, for the Scarab Occult saw it as their duty to guard the forbidden knowledge their Primarch had collected. The Rubric of Ahriman sealed each warrior inside his defiled armour permanently, locking the remnants of their souls for eternity with the idolatrous spell-words they had etched. Over millennia of exposure to the warp, the true power of these etchings has blended with the essence of each warrior, creating in the Scarab Occult a hellishly twisted warrior cabal.

Their armour has retained much of its potency over the long centuries since their creation. Refractor-field generators have become saturated with empyric energy, causing the air around them to writhe as incoming fire is deflected harmlessly. Each suit is also capable of withstanding the pressures of teleportation, allowing the warriors of the Scarab Occult to emerge suddenly onto the battlefield through holes torn in reality.

The ubiquitous weapon of the Scarab Occult Terminators is a cruelly curved blade based on the khopesh of ancient Prospero. The earliest khopeshes were forged from what scant pieces of precious metals could be found on the barren world, and were symbols of authority used to mete out punishment to those who disobeyed Prosperine laws. When the Thousand Sons Legion came to Prospero, the khopesh was adopted by the Scarab Occult as the mark of their rank, and they were fitted with power-field generators to allow them to cleave matter at a molecular level. Though the warriors of the Scarab Occult are but ghosts of their former glory, the deadly speed and skill with which they wield their blades in close quarters has remained ever potent.

# BESTIAL HORDES

Where the Thousand Sons pledged their souls to Tzeentch or were manipulated into his service, fighting alongside them are those who are born of the Great Shaper's hideous will. These creatures are a fusion of bestial ferocity, avian agility and human cunning, and by raw instinct they sow the seeds of mutation throughout the galaxy.

## TZAANGORS

The blasphemous chanting of massed Tzaangors rises to a crescendo as they draw close to their prey. Multi-hued tongues flap within aquiline beaks, eagerly lapping up the taste of fear and confusion. Iridescent eyes glow with inhuman savagery, and the cruelly twisted horns that sprout from each Tzaangor's skull clatter together as they vie to be first into the fray. With jagged blades they hack their victims apart before trampling the dying beneath clawed feet.

Tzaangors are the mutated bearers of Tzeentch's blessings, unnatural abominations who serve as shock troops for the Thousand Sons thrallbands. Their bodies, though hideously malformed by the warping power of the Architect of Fate, are ideally suited to warfare. Long limbs flex with corded muscle, and thorny quill-like protrusions grow across their chests and shoulders. Most Tzaangors resemble some sort of amalgam of man, beast and bird, although some are even more aberrant in shape, with heads that are split down the middle or bodies rent with fluctuating clefts.

The origins of Tzaangors are as varied as their appearance. They arise where Tzeentch wills it, and are brought into being by his blessed transmutations. Some are the product of grim experiments performed on the slaves taken to the Planet of the Sorcerers. Others are shaped from the crews of damaged ships caught in warp storms, their bodies transmuted through exposure to pure empyric power. Perhaps most horrific are the Tzaangors born to human mothers on worlds enshrouded by the Cicatrix Maledictum. Whole generations of these creatures burst quickly into nightmarish existence, whereupon they ravenously devour the defenders of their home planet.

Tzaangors are driven by warp-infused compulsion to seek out knowledge in all its forms, and to slaughter those who stand in the way of their pursuits. Alongside these predatory instincts exists a level of cunning and intelligence belied by their monstrous form. Tzaangors are more than capable of formulating complex battle plans, communicating amongst their ranks through harsh trills and staccato clicks. Working together in flocks, they can run ruin through an unsuspecting populace or entrenched enemy line. Each Tzaangor is motivated by a personal desire to accumulate arcane knowledge, and it is their belief that through the pursuit of such knowledge they may receive even more of Tzeentch's blessings.

To enact their butchery, some Tzaangors wield massive blades wrought from metal or bone, while others use buzzing chainswords and crude autopistols. Often, a member of a flock will carry a daemonically mawed instrument, the piercing blasts of which stir other nearby Tzaangors into a bestial frenzy. The most savage member of a flock is known as a Twistbray, and they usually bear on their body the most warping gifts of their creator-god.

## TZAANGOR ENLIGHTENED

Tzaangors whose hunt for knowledge has caught the eye of their god may be bestowed one of Tzeentch's blessings. Often this results in the creature devolving into an even more grotesque abomination – a Chaos Spawn. However, the lucky few engorged with such warp power are elevated above their twisted brethren, physically, mentally and spiritually. They exist in a state of constant communion with Tzeentch, and through him they see the shifting strands of fate converge and separate.

The Tzaangors view the Enlightened as paragons of warfare, and the destiny towards which they all must progress. Enlightened soar above the battlefield on Discs of Tzeentch, riding the streams of fate as a raptor would ride thermals. Even the Sorcerers of the Thousand Sons respect these creatures, for their savagery is seen as one of Tzeentch's many esoteric tools. Constantly aware of the flow of causality, Enlightened can see where and when their strikes will cause the most damage. The divining spears some carry are tuned to predetermined victims, emitting humming reverberations that grow louder as they near their targets. Other Enlightened wield fatecaster greatbows, strung with ectoplasmic cords that send ensorcelled arrows on deadly paths. Lastly, some carry chainswords and autopistols used in their past lives as human heretics, for these were the tools by which they first achieved glory before Tzeentch.

## TZAANGOR SHAMANS

Tzaangor Shamans are the most exalted of their mutated kind. They are oracles and prophets, and they preach to their ilk atop flying Discs of Tzeentch. Their psychic mastery is born not of endless study, but of singular devotion to their god, and is unleashed upon their foes amidst ritual chants in the fathomless language of the Tzaangors. It is with the Shamans that the Sorcerers of the Thousand Sons make their fell pacts, though these Sorcerers are ever wary of the deals they make; the Shamans serve the fickle will of Tzeentch above all else.

On the Planet of the Sorcerers, Shamans lead herds of their kin on long pilgrimages across the constantly shifting warp-wastes. These mass migrations follow lines of power that wind across the planet's crust, converging at sites where the roiling aetheric energy is at its thickest. At these sites, they raise great flux-cairns – megaliths inscribed with glyphs and runes, and shaped in symbols sacred to Tzeentch – which serve as repositories for the arcane knowledge stolen and despoiled by the Tzaangor tribes. The Shamans use these to channel Tzeentch's power throughout realspace by erecting duplicate monoliths in the jungles and barrens of other worlds. The longer each simulacra remains in place, the more its warping influence bleeds into the planet on which it stands, transforming the world and preparing it for a full-scale invasion.

*'Every abomination is a creation of Tzeentch. Every twisted monstrosity a child of the Changer of Ways. If I could, I would devour the thoughts of them all, that I too might know the horror of their existence. But for me there is a different fate.'*

*- Hasophet, Magister of the Mind-Eaters*

# CHAOS CULTISTS

Of the heaving masses that make up the citizenry of the Imperium, most live in desperate squalor, packed into mountainous hive cities where they toil endlessly in vast manufactorums. Generations upon generations live and die in a state of constant fear – fear of invasion, fear of starvation, and fear of the retribution they will face if they dare to cast off the shackles of Imperial order. These wretched conditions are the perfect breeding ground for dissent and rebellion. In the face of hopelessness, many are swayed by whispered stories that tell of the Chaos Gods and the rewards bestowed upon their followers. Such unimaginable power is tantalising to the powerless, and sets many on the path to damnation.

> 'This was my hand! It was ripped from my wrist three tithes ago in the teeth of a forging press. Our oppressors seared my severed stump so that I could remain at my station without bleeding to death. But look upon my hand now, sisters and brothers! It has regrown, and with more fingers than I could ever have hoped for. It is a blessing from the Great Saviour, and such blessings can be yours also. All that is required of you is faith.'
>
> - Grekk Redeye, Sermon in the Sump

Cults begin to grow deep within the fabric of Imperial worlds, driven by the profane preachings of Chaos-touched demagogues. Though many of these cults are found and eradicated by the Ordo Hereticus, the watchers within the Imperium are not able to have eyes everywhere, and many more of these cults flourish. The Cultists hide in plain sight, their drab clothes covering tattoos and symbols they have carved into their own flesh, dedicated to the ruinous powers. Their numbers continue to swell with time until the cult has infected large portions of the planet's society, and a collective feeling of destiny gives the members purpose. They begin to gather weapons into secret caches, pilfering from planetary defence forces and crafting makeshift implements with which they can hack and bludgeon. Some are even given visions which reveal methods to piece together crude but effective guns.

As their hour of reckoning approaches, the most faithful servants are marked with hideous mutations, and the wretches that behold these gifts offer up their souls willingly in worship to Tzeentch.

At last, as the invading forces of the Thousand Sons approach their world, the Cultists' presence is unveiled. In a violent explosion of pent-up wrath they fall upon those with whom they have lived their whole lives. None are spared from their twisted fury, and they carve great bloody swathes through the hab-blocks and manufactorum districts, chanting blasphemies and paradoxical oaths as they rampage. Giant pyres are lit in the name of Tzeentch, and by their burning light the Cultists continue to mangle and mutilate those still loyal to the Imperium.

Many cities – even whole worlds – fall quickly to the sudden influx of Cultists, their defences completely overrun by the seemingly unending flood of bodies. But those that somehow are able to stem the tide of violence face an even greater threat, as the thrallbands of the Thousand Sons begin their inexorable march. Inferno bolt fire and crackling beams of eldritch energy fly over the teeming throngs of Cultists, while tanks and Daemon Engines tear through ferrocrete walls to allow the stampede of tainted Humanity to continue. The sheer volume of Cultists allows them to soak up a vast amount of returned fire without losing momentum, and the sight of Rubric Marines and Sorcerers on the battlefield sends them into a religious fervour – for these ornately armoured Chaos Space Marines are like walking saints, come to bless the Cultists for their loyal devotion.

Whatever hope a Cultist may have derived from their profane worship is inevitably false. They are but pawns in the plans of the Thousand Sons, meat to clog the wheels of the Imperial war machine. Should they live through their initial uprising, no great reward awaits them. Those who survive may be taken by the thrallbands to other war zones where they will again be sent to die on the front lines. Others are transported to the Planet of the Sorcerers to serve as slaves or to be used as subjects in arcane experiments. Others are simply overtaken by their own mutations, and become gibbering Chaos Spawn.

# CHAOS SPAWN

All of the Chaos Gods are generous with their gifts of mutation, but none more so than Tzeentch, Changer of the Ways. As Tzeentch's mortal champions continue to serve their dark master, they are rewarded with ever more bizarre and horrific transformations. A Sorcerer's hands may morph into many-tentacled appendages, all the better suited to performing complex rites of spellcraft. Their eyes may become liquefied orbs capable of seeing the tangled lines of fate that guide a battle. Each of these gifts is a mark of favour, and a step closer to the ultimate goal of ascension to true daemonhood. But for every mortal soul that is forged into a powerful warp creature, countless others are deemed unworthy. Their flesh is bent into the tortured form of a Chaos Spawn, a hideous monster driven by madness to endless acts of depraved violence.

Chaos Spawn are as varied in shape as the plans and schemes of the Great Manipulator himself. The body from which the Spawn pupates grows vast with layers of muscle and sagging flab, enveloping the contorted skeleton and rapidly mutating organs within. Limbs elongate and multiply, fracturing along their length to allow for new movement before developing sharply articulated joints. Claws and bony protrusions sprout from deep within the creature's musculature, and internal tissues burst forth to form flapping, mucous-covered pseudopods. This biology is utterly incapable of sustaining a natural existence, yet it is given fuel by the unquenchable insanity of the being that has been transformed, for in his infinite wisdom Tzeentch allows the unfortunate mortal to retain just enough of their former intellect to experience an eternity of madness.

The Thousand Sons view Chaos Spawn as a natural by-product of their quests for knowledge and arcane superiority. These abominations aimlessly roam the surface of the Planet of the Sorcerers, formed from those whose aspirations led them to pursue empyric power for which they were not worthy. In their arrogance, few Sorcerers believe that such a hideous transmogrification will be their fate, and they are more than willing to use the twisted creatures to achieve their own ends. Droves of Chaos Spawn are kept in enormous pens in Tizca, their endless inhuman screams reverberating through

the city until the twisted beasts are taken to some distant war zone.

A Chaos Spawn is incapable of reason, and so must be herded into battle by more esoteric means. A Sorcerer may place a series of wards to funnel the Spawn's spasmodic movements towards the lines of their enemy; or they may simply array slaves in a line across the battlefield, trusting the creature's pained instincts to drive it from one victim to the next until it reaches the intended foe.

Once the Chaos Spawn is in battle there is no more need to guide its movements, for it will slash savagely with grotesque claws and barbed horns until no living creature stands in its path. The mutations that wrack its body render its flailing attacks impossible to predict, with newly formed blades jutting from its flesh to skewer those nearby and gouts of toxic fluid erupting from its innards to melt flesh from bone. Such variegated carnage is pleasing to Tzeentch, and in this way the Chaos Spawn continues to serve its cruel creator.

# MUTALITH VORTEX BEASTS

No creature embodies the warped will of Tzeentch more than the Mutalith Vortex Beast. These nightmarish monstrosities are as large as they are twisted, towering above infantry and even tanks as they bound across the battlefield. Their thunderous roar reverberates for miles in every direction, piercing the psyche of all in earshot and filling their minds' eyes with visions of paradoxical horror. Yet this projected terror is surpassed by the reality of the Mutalith Vortex Beast crashing into the enemy army. Its rippling musculature grows, splits and reknits as the creature thrashes violently. Massive razor-jagged claws shred through tank armour, exposing those inside to the aura of ravaging flux that surrounds the Vortex Beast. From its betentacled maw, tendrils formed from warp-putrefied inner organs flap voraciously outwards, tearing infantry limb from limb or constricting the hapless victims before drawing their crushed bodies deep inside the monster's mashing gullet.

The formation of a Mutalith Vortex Beast is an entirely unnatural process, yet they can be brought into being by the currents of warp energy that flow over the surface of the Planet of the Sorcerers. Often, this occurs when dozens of Chaos Spawn get caught in an empyric eddy and are fused together by the swirl of raw magic. These abominable conglomerations typically perish quickly, collapsing under the weight of their own incongruous form into a quivering mound of warp-infused ooze.

But on occasion, the will of Tzeentch binds the hyper-mutated flesh and bone together into a monstrous composite far more deadly than the sum of its hideous parts.

Over the millennia, many Sorcerers have attempted to create their own Mutalith Vortex Beast with obscure spells to induce the gross transformation. Even when such an invocation succeeds, more often than not the Sorcerer is consumed by their own magic, their flesh being added to the writhing matter of their creation. Other Mutalith Vortex Beasts are formed from supremely powerful Sorcerers who, at the moment they believe they have achieved daemonhood, fall victim to the cruel whims of their fickle patron.

The hulking body of a Vortex Beast acts as an empyric reservoir, drawing in and absorbing Chaos energy. This energy saturates the creature's flesh, at once holding its impossible anatomy together and tearing it apart. The constant struggle between entropy and coalescence creates a swirling psychic tempest around the Mutalith Vortex Beast – a storm of flux power that engulfs all who draw near, steadily warping their existence. The Sorcerers of the Thousand Sons revel in this change-field, watching with great pleasure as realspace is racked by strange mutations. As the Vortex Beast's flesh is torn open by cannon fire and hacking blades, torrents of unreleased power bleed onto the battlefield, causing ever more anarchic fluctuations in reality.

Before herding a Mutalith Vortex Beast to battle, the Thousand Sons harness the creature with a giant pointed star made of fire taken from atop the Tower of the Cyclops. Bound within this burning Chaos icon is an orb – a fractured piece of the great eye that crowns Magnus' tower – and through this burning portal the raging Chaos winds from the Planet of the Sorcerers are channelled, allowing the raw power of the Thousand Sons' world to seep freely onto the battlefield.

# BATTLE TANKS

Housed in the towers on the Planet of the Sorcerers are heavily armoured vehicles whose machine spirits have been twisted by dark sorceries to serve the Thousand Sons. When called to battle, these war engines launch formidable salvoes of fire and ferry the Legion's infantry to where they can unleash the most devastation upon the enemy.

## CHAOS RHINOS

With their engines emitting a ceaseless metallic scream, spearheads of Chaos Rhinos barrel across the battlefield to deliver their payload into the heart of the enemy line. Thick ablative plating shields the warriors within the twisted transport bay from incoming shots, allowing Rubricae, Cultists or snarling Tzaangors to be swiftly redeployed across the field of war as the battle plans of their sorcerous masters shift and change.

## CHAOS PREDATORS

Chaos Predators are rumbling engines of war, capable of laying down devastating barrages of long-range firepower. Their various armaments make them equally deadly when facing packed ranks of infantry or enemy armour, and when deployed in force they can obliterate an opposing line in a matter of moments. Equally, they can send defenders rushing desperately for cover, allowing a Sorcerer time to infuse the battlefield with their dark magic.

## CHAOS VINDICATORS

The robust chassis of the Chaos Vindicator is fitted with an enormous front-mounted shield, making it a consummate siege engine. Those of the Thousand Sons plough defiantly through the throng of battle, and from the front lines lob massive shells from their demolisher cannons into the heart of the enemy formation. Along with flesh and rubble, the detonation of these shells sends iridescent trails of sorcerous energy streaming through the air.

## CHAOS LAND RAIDERS

A Chaos Land Raider of the Thousand Sons is a behemoth of adamantium and plasteel, its armoured hide mutating as its multitudinous gun-mounts shift to track their targets. Its front hatch yawns open to expose a vast transport bay, within which the fiercest warriors of the Legion – Scarab Occult Terminators – can be carried to battle. The rarity of these vehicles means that only the most powerful sects can deploy them for war.

# HELBRUTES

Like the Dreadnoughts used by the loyalist Adeptus Astartes, Helbrutes are walking engines of war driven by the fallen warrior entombed within their hull. But unlike the Imperial walkers – each an honoured relic of their Chapter – Helbrutes are viewed with hatred by the living warriors of the Thousand Sons, for each is an implement of eternal torture, a machine designed to transform the suffering of its unwilling inhabitant into unquenchable rage.

Helbrutes are entirely symbiotic, requiring a sacrificial mind and body to achieve animus. The first of the Thousand Sons Helbrutes were created when those Traitor Legionaries who were locked within Dreadnoughts were wracked by mutation on the Planet of the Sorcerers. But flesh is harder to come by in the Legion now. The disembodied Rubricae lack the physical and spiritual substance required to fuel the Helbrutes' hungering engines. As such, Sorcerers weave complex schemes to bait Chaos Space Marines of other Legions into their cabals. These foreign warriors are promised powers beyond imagining and mastery over the vast array of knowledge the Thousand Sons have harvested. They are given tutelage in the ways of the psyker – or so they believe. In truth, each trial they undertake is another step in the ritualistic binding of their soul to the Helbrute's machinery. The surges of power felt by the hopeful supplicant are in fact the first twitches of warp-connectivity between their mutating neurons and the arcane servo-relays of the Chaos walker. Only when the ritual is beyond reversing does the victim become aware of their inescapable fate.

The sacrificial warrior is flensed and reduced with warpflame to a pulped mass of organs, bones and nervous tissue. Throughout this process, the crafting Sorcerer keeps their subject psychically tethered to the roaring engines of the Helbrute, forcing them to remain conscious through the agony of their transformation. The victim is then placed in an amniotic sac, which in turn is inserted into the coffin-like maw of the Helbrute. This is the tomb in which the sacrificed warrior will experience an agonised existence seemingly without end.

The torment of the warrior inside the amniotic sac is fused to the Helbrute's motivators; his unquenchable hatred for those who deceived him hard-wired into the war machine's cogitation arrays. The metal cage that holds the warrior's remains melds with his flesh, turning man and machine into a single psychotic organism. From this point, the interred Chaos Space Marine is bound to his maddening agony. Only by tearing savagely into the enemies of the Sorcerer who controls him can the machine-warrior hope to find the sweet release of oblivion.

With monstrous, metallic howls the Helbrute wades into combat, blasting foes into gobbets of flesh from afar or swinging its weapon arms in deadly arcs to pulverise the champions of the enemy army. In the moments before each kill, the screaming consciousness of the Helbrute believes it will receive some relief from its anguish in seeing others suffer, but its thirst for numbness is never satisfied. Where the interred warrior once sought knowledge, he is now denied all thought but the consciousness of his own wretched existence, driving him to ever greater heights of madness and ever more brutal acts of battlefield violence.

Between battles the Helbrute is locked in the depths of the Thousand Sons' armouries, where the flesh sac is wrenched painfully from its sarcophagus. Through a web of sorcerous wards, the lumpen being is given sense enough to feel the raw horror of empyric currents flowing through its dungeon cell, and the pain of re-entwining the warrior with its machine body increases exponentially with each iteration. In this way, the Helbrute's insanity is maintained even when not in battle – a necessity to ensure that its violent psychosis is never dulled.

# HELDRAKES

Heldrakes are a savage breed of Daemon Engine, borne to battle on enormous metallic wings. In their appearance and savagery, they resemble the great wyrms slain by the warriors of the Thousand Sons when they first entered the warp and claimed the Planet of the Sorcerers. Of all the Daemon Engines, Heldrakes are held in the highest regard by the Sons of Magnus, for they are seen as embodiments of the fiery serpent that has long been the symbol of Tzeentch's servants.

As the ranks of Rubric Marines make their lockstep marches towards the enemy, Heldrakes swoop overhead with terrifying speed. Opposing fighter craft are torn from the sky with each cruel sweep of the Heldrake's twisted metal claws. Wings and vector thrusters are ripped from the flyers' chassis, sending the crippled vehicles plummeting to the ground below to explode like burning meteors amidst their allies. Following close behind the falling wreckage, the Heldrake spews hails of bullets or gouts of immolating flames from its savage jaws, raking across the enemy formation. Those not cut down or incinerated often turn and flee in abject terror from the winged monster, but few are the prey swift enough to outrun it. With its quarry strewn bloodily before it, the Heldrake takes to the air once more with a mighty pounce, quickly sighting where next it can wreak ruin.

Only the most erudite amongst the Thousand Sons know the grim truth of the Heldrakes – that they were once the Legion's fighter craft. The pilots that flew these craft survived the Rubric of Ahriman only to be subsumed by their war engines, although many welcomed this transformation as a blessing from the God of Change and gave their souls willingly to take on the glorious, draconic form of the Heldrake.

The harrowing transmutation from aerial fighter to soaring Daemon Engine drove the pilots beyond the brink of sanity. Predatory entities clawed their way inside each vehicle, where they corrupted the craft's machine spirits with their warp essence. The pilots were also mutated by the presence, their genetically enhanced bodies becoming indistinguishable from the cockpits in which they sat. Their senses combined with those of their craft, so that all they could see, hear and smell came through the vehicles' auspex arrays, and damage inflicted upon the monstrous machines was also felt in their own diminishing bodies. Their minds were riven by incomprehensible Tzeentchian consciousnesses, who morphed the crafts to shapes more fitting their natures. Eventually, the pilots were reduced to vestigial hearts at the core of each Heldrake, pumping not blood but malice and contempt through the Daemon Engines' aetheric veins.

# DAEMON ENGINES

Daemon Engines are hulking metallic monsters given animus by the warp entities caged within their twisted frames. The Thousand Sons do not create Daemon Engines – instead, they procure the bestial machines through pacts with the Dark Mechanicum, or use fell sorceries to bind the creations of other Legions to their own malevolent purposes.

## DEFILERS

As the Defiler stalks across the battlefield, the very ground around it heaves and screams under the weight of daemonic energy radiating from its arachnoid form. With every grinding movement, its many-jointed limbs send out ripples of warping force, filling the minds of all who behold the mechanical creature with unrelenting dread. Its fore-claws gouge the earth, helping to haul the immense bulk of the Defiler onwards towards its prey, before thrusting forwards to tear through defensive barricades and mutilate the enemy's ranks. It is a metallic abomination, born of the demented minds of the followers of Chaos, and put to hideous use by the Thousand Sons as a walking engine of devastation.

Atop the crawling legs, the Defiler's torso is an armoured fortress from which multifarious armaments protrude. Bursting from its chest, its battle cannon launches high-explosive shells with thundering force, and can rupture the armoured vehicles of the enemy with a single well-placed shot. Like the Defiler itself, each of the cannon's shells has become host to a Tzeentchian entity. As the warhead explodes, the released Lesser Daemon warps the shape of reality within the blast radius, sending chunks of shrapnel, rock and bone flying. Ever bound to their prison, the entity then coalesces back in the Defiler's hull, there to reform as another shell waiting to be fired upon another target.

Even if an enemy force is able to disable a Defiler by inflicting irreparable damage, its death throes can be catastrophic. The Daemon may burst free from its cage in a violent eruption of raw warp energy, producing an unfettered empyric shock wave which can cause armour to fold in upon itself, organs to spontaneously ignite and weapons to explode in the hands of their wielders. As the raging Daemon revels in its liberation, it begins to evaporate, seeping swiftly back to the immaterial plane. The sudden backwash of warp-essence strips flesh from bone and can disintegrate adamantium at a molecular level.

The Defiler's upper limbs can be fitted with different armaments, allowing it to spit out hails of rapid fire, swarms of missiles or blasts of crackling las-energy. Some Defilers instead bear enormous scourging flails that swing and spin with incredible speed, shredding armour and flesh with equal ease. Each of these weapons allows a Defiler to wreak different forms of destruction upon the battlefield. Amongst most Traitor Legions, a Defiler is created with a single set of killing tools, for the Daemon inside the machine merges also with its weapons, becoming part of them and they part of it. But those Defilers used by the Thousand Sons are creatures of Tzeentch, and are more amenable to shifting forms and varied methods of brutality. Yet even with a Tzeentchian Daemon riddling the war engine, the rituals to separate the Defiler's body parts and replace them with others are arduous and fraught with danger. Such a task is usually undertaken by a large cabal of Aspiring Sorcerers, and few survive the process. The portion of the Daemon's essence residing in the weapon is drawn out and held in the minds of the cabal. If one of them falters, the fragmented warp entity swiftly ravages the psyches of them all, but if they

are able to maintain their sanity for hours, days or even weeks, the uninhabited weapon will slough off the Defiler's hull. A new weapon, carved with runes bearing the true name of the entrapped entity, can then be affixed to the shifting metal body, and the daemonic fragment is allowed to return to its altered cage.

Due to their sheer destructive capabilities, Defilers are highly sought after by the Exalted Sorcerers of the Legion's many sects. These warlords are often given visions of the worlds they could set ablaze with but a handful of the Daemon Engines joined to their thrallbands. Driven by these prophecies they lay complex plans to deceive and influence the Warpsmiths of other Chaos Legions into binding Daemon and machine in the most devastating of configurations. The ambition of the Warpsmiths is their greatest weakness, and the Exalted Sorcerers guide their actions, making them believe they are fulfilling some gods-given task of profane fabrication. When the Warpsmith's grotesque work is complete, the Thousand Sons arrive to claim the fruit of his labour. The creator is butchered, burned or fed as a first offering to his Daemon Engine, then the rites are begun to bind the Defiler to its new master.

## FORGEFIENDS

Like a great lumbering beast, the Forgefiend tromps across the battlefield, its piston-like legs shattering the earth beneath its massive weight. The Daemon sown into the machine emits its deafening howls through metallic grills before opening fire, blasting bodies to pieces and vehicles to slag. Though a Forgefiend resembles a monstrous beast in appearance – a terrifying predator at the apex of some death world's food chain – its instincts are not those of an animal, but of a malevolent empyric entity. It is motivated to hunt by spite and pure hatred, spitting long-range death at its prey on the battlefield.

The foundries used to create Forgefiends lie on worlds where swirling Chaos matter can readily be drawn upon. Warpfire furnaces blaze with the heat of suns, for only in such conditions can Daemons be bound within their eternal metal cages. Into this inferno the Warpsmiths pour their sorcerous energies, sacrificing portions of their own sanity to realise their blasphemous designs. When the body of a Forgefiend has been shaped and the Daemon entity sealed within, the Tzeentchian fire used to fuse the two together continues to rage in the amalgam-creature's core. Unquenchable and ever-changing, this flame provides the reservoir of warp power to which the Forgefiend gives destructive form.

Some Forgefiends bear on their bestial frontal limbs a pair of hades autocannons, heavy six-barrelled guns that lay down sawing lines of solid shot. Each of the hundreds of bullets fired per minute is a crystallised strand of the Forgefiend's blazing internal warpfire, and they crackle through the air before searing their way through enemy armour and infantry ranks. The barrels scream as they disgorge their unnatural payload, spitting out thick clouds of iridescent smoke that quickly fill the battlefield with a choking fume.

Other Forgefiends have clawed limbs that open as gaping maws to vomit globules of empyric matter over their targets. These cannons are a twisted perversion of ancient Imperial plasma technology, and draw upon the Forgefiend's own unstable energy reserve rather than relying on an external power core. With every searing discharge, an ectoplasma cannon lobs an orb of warp-matter saturated with the unquiet remains of lesser entities that have been absorbed by the Daemon within the Forgefiend.

Forgefiends are filled with jealous contempt for the unbound Daemons of Tzeentch. Such Daemons exist to exert their will freely, to create change and flux by the outpouring of their own essence. Confined inside their mechanical exoskeleton, a Forgefiend is greatly limited in the fulfilment of this existence. The Thousand Sons know that this is torture to these Daemons, and they use this torture to their advantage, for a Forgefiend will allow the fires inside themselves to erupt whenever they get the chance, raining many-formed destruction upon whatever enemies are lured into their sights.

## MAULERFIENDS

Maulerfiends are anarchic siege engines, created to rampage ahead of a thrallband's march where they can wreak the most havoc. With warp-infused servos driving their enormous forelimbs, a Maulerfiend can build up terrifying speed and momentum, stomping over piles of smouldering wreckage and mounds of corpses before crashing into defensive fortifications. Their clawed

fists make quick work of ferrocrete barricades, allowing the machine-beast to continue on its warpath, mashing its way through infantry and vehicles with equal disregard.

Many Sorcerers deploy Maulerfiends armed with magma cutters to eviscerate opposing columns of armour before they even reach the main battlefield. Through a magma cutter, the Daemon bound within the Maulerfiend can focus its searing breath into a short-range beam of heat that can slice open thick ablative armour. At other times, when the divinations of the Thousand Sons have shown that they will face dense packs of footsoldiers, they loose before them Maulerfiends fitted with lasher tendrils. These thick, tentacle-like cables thrash violently and erratically, whipping with lightning speed and transforming whole ranks of enemy troops into crimson clouds of blood and viscera. Though lasher tendrils are usually forged from liquefactive metals, on some Maulerfiends they have morphed into barbed strands of aetheric matter or mutated biological appendages.

A thrallband will often carve cryptic runes on a Maulerfiend to bend the Daemon within to their specific purpose. In their battles with the Necrons of the Nephrekh Dynasty, the Silver Sons forged sigils that filled their Maulerfiends with a rapacious hunger for metal. The machine-beasts thundered through the enemy lines, tearing the metallic warriors limb from limb. Even when the Necrons reassembled themselves, the warp energy emanating from the slavering Daemon Engines caused them to reconstitute as twisted, inviable conglomerations of mismatching body parts.

# DAEMONS OF TZEENTCH

**Daemons are creatures of the aether given form by the Chaos Gods. Those born of Tzeentch's will are entities of unbridled mutation, agents of change in service to the Architect of Fate. Through profane rituals and dark entreaties they are summoned to the battlefield by the Sorcerers of the Thousand Sons, where their unnatural existence strikes terror into the minds of the sane.**

## HORRORS

The most abundant of Tzeentch's children are his hordes of Pink, Blue and Brimstone Horrors. From the globular bodies of these psuedo-beings sprout multiple limbs contorted into strange angles alongside flapping tentacular appendages. Their slash-like mouths may be jagged with irregular rows of fangs or protrude into cruel beaks, and their long tongues undulate with incantations of incomprehensible blasphemy.

The largest of these Lesser Daemons are the Pink Horrors. They lollop to combat in a constant state of unnatural exuberance, eagerly leaping over one another to reach the enemy, or to draw closer to a site of power on the battlefield. From the midst of their frolicking masses come streamers of coruscating flame to incinerate their foes, and blasts of mutative energy that ravage those unfaithful to their father-creator.

Though seemingly separate creatures, each Pink Horror is an extension of Tzeentch's many-faceted will, and they operate as one to channel the energies of the warp. As children of the Changer of the Ways, Pink Horrors are prone to sudden and drastic fluctuations. In fact, should a Pink Horror be grievously wounded, its essence will not drain immediately back to the immaterium but instead it splits in two, becoming a duo of Blue Horrors. In stark contrast to the gleeful being from which they emerged, Blue Horrors are dour and mirthless. They bound forwards not with gaiety, but with dark intent, tearing at those they approach with scrabbling teeth and claws.

Should a Blue Horror be cut down or blasted apart in its turn, the creature will emit a long, drawn-out and fatalistic groan before vanishing in a cloud of acrid smoke. From out of these unnatural fumes emerge a pair of Daemons smaller still – two tiny Brimstone Horrors. These diminutive fiends have bodies made of flickering fire, and from them the pungent stench of sulphur wafts across the battlefield. Each is but a fractured speck of spiteful emotion, a psychotic fleeting thought given form, and they burn bright before fizzling from existence. In the brief time before a Brimstone Horror evaporates back to the warp, it hungers for flesh and minds which its hateful essence can burn.

Horrors cannot exist naturally outside of the warp, and the rituals that summon them cannot sustain their existence in realspace for long. As daemonic creatures, they are anathema to reality, and the very air around them scintillates, sometimes showing maddening glimpses of various pasts and futures. They do not experience anything approaching mortal fear, though they bleed from reality when faced with overwhelming opposition.

## SCREAMERS

The broad-winged Daemons known as Screamers swim through the vast sea of the immaterium in great shoals, racing through aetheric eddies and warp currents without slowing. In their wake they leave trails of iridescent light, and all around them echo the mind-piercing shrieks that give them their name.

Screamers are pack hunters that can locate the psychic and emotional scent of a mortal being's warp shadow across manifold planes of existence. They pursue these scents relentlessly, tracking their targets before descending to shred them, body and mind. Even a Geller field – the protective bubble that protects a ship in warp transit from the wrath of malefic entities – cannot fully blunt the psychic spoor that draws schools of Screamers. Screamers have been known to burrow through the Geller fields of craft they find adrift, peeling open the hull and allowing Chaos energy to flood the ship. As those inside flounder and choke, their own mutating anatomies squeezing them of their life, the Screamers pour in to devour the crew in their last terrified moments of existence.

Shoals of Screamers are drawn to battles in realspace where panic and confusion hang thick in the air. The Sorcerers of the Thousand Sons expedite the Daemons' arrival with rituals that open direct portals to the Screamers' usual feeding grounds. From these the abominations swoop into reality, ignoring the laws of gravity and effects of atmospheric conditions that can hamper other flying creatures. As the Screamers fly across the battlefield their lashing tails whip down to impale those below with brutal barbs. Those not bisected or disembowelled outright are weakened physically and spiritually, and are marked by the Screamers as a later meal.

## FLAMERS

With impossible physiologies that can drive those who behold them insane, Flamers are amongst the most perplexing servants of Tzeentch. They float to war surrounded by an aura of reality-mutating madness that twists gravity itself, allowing them to bound effortlessly over their enemies. Despite their grotesquely misshapen forms they are surprisingly agile, swiftly swooping through the air to land close to their next unfortunate victim.

A Flamer's body is riven with hideous maws that gape wide, seal closed and then reopen elsewhere. From each of these maws drip aetheric flames made of pure warp magic. The maws bite and gnash, but only while the Flamer is preparing its most deadly attack, for with a great convulsion the Daemon can spray its reservoir of flame outwards. Most unlike any naturally occurring fire, this flame pours forth in a flickering torrent, rushing like a tidal wave towards its target.

Rather than incinerating with heat, Flamers disfigure and transmute those their fires envelop. Their targets undergo thousands of changes, their muscles, bones, organs and wargear melding into one another then apart again, constantly reconfiguring. Lungs balloon out and wrap around themselves, vocal cords wind into fractal shapes and vox-grills become living organs wired to the pain centres of the victim's mutating brain. At last, when the flames cease, whatever haphazard conglomeration of matter remains is completely unable to support its own existence – the victim crumbles into dust or sloughs into a puddle of ooze. Some Flamers spew fire that warps the psyche of the victim, transforming their memories and immolating every vestige of their mind, whereas others burn the very souls of those they ignite.

# AGENTS OF CHANGE

When the Thousand Sons march to war, they do so wreathed in warpfire and sorcerous lightning. Their armour and heraldry is emblazoned with baleful runes dedicated to Tzeentch, alongside the symbols of their cult and thrallband.

**Ahriman riding a Disc of Tzeentch**

The earth writhes and cracks as Magnus the Red approaches. Beneath the shadow of his wings his warriors unleash waves of inferno bolts to cut down the Grey Knights who seek to banish the Daemon Primarch to the warp once more.

'In your service to me there is no excuse for failure. If time is against you, bend it to your will. If portents of the future bode ill, wrench that path of fate from existence and forge your destiny anew.'

- Magnus the Red,
speaking to the Rehati in Tizca

When he marches to war, Magnus brings with him his dread tome of arcane knowledge.

Magnus the Red, Daemon Primarch of the Thousand Sons

Exalted Sorcerers with force staves on Discs of Tzeentch

Exalted Sorcerers with force staves

'When I look before the Rubric, I see myself blindly stumbling through war after war, my eye closed to the future and unaware of my own destiny. My mind was not ready, and I could not hope to understand the power which I now possess. To behold this past is like looking into a mirror that has been blackened by fire. The self I see is a dim reflection who believes falsely that he controls his own fate. But when I move to wipe away the soot, my reflection moves his hand also. He is and always was a puppet, and I am now the puppeteer. It was by my own hand that I was guided to my current greatness, and from the future I can hear an even greater self whispering to me now. His words are not yet known to me, but I can already feel the heat of the glorious infernos which I will one day ignite in my own name.'

*- Manat, Exalted Sorcerer of the Cult of Time*

**Aspiring Sorcerer**

**Rubric Marine with
Icon of Flame**

**Rubric Marine with
soulreaper cannon**

**Rubric Marine with
inferno boltgun**

**Rubric Marine
with warpflamer**

**Rubric Marine with
inferno boltgun**

**Chaos Rhino with combi-bolter**

Ahriman lures a Space Wolves strike force and a Culexus Assassin to the industrial wastes of an Imperial hive world. Their immolation will provide the flesh sacrifice required for his latest rite of divination.

Shown here are a number of colour schemes for a Thousand Sons army. These depict but a small fraction of the manifold sects that comprise the Legion.

**Rubric Marine of the Crimson Sons**

**Rubric Marine of the Sectai Prosperine**

**Rubric Marine of the Thralls of Magnus**

**Rubric Marine of the Hermetic Blades**

**Scarab Occult Terminator of the Blades of Magnus**

As Magnus sends waves of automata-like Rubricae against the hulking machines of the Adeptus Mechanicus, the air fills with the din of binharic cant and profane invocations.

**Converted Sorcerer in Terminator Armour with force stave and power sword**

**Helbrute with Helbrute plasma cannon and Helbrute hammer**

**Tzaangors with chainswords and autopistols**

**Tzaangor Enlightened**

**Tzaangor Shaman**

**Scarab Occult Sorcerer with
force stave and power sword**

**Scarab Occult Terminators**

**Scarab Occult Terminator with
soulreaper cannon**

**Scarab Occult Terminator
with hellfyre missile rack**

**Scarab Occult Terminator
with inferno-combi bolter**

# ACOLYTES OF TZEENTCH

The Sons of Magnus have access to a large number of psykers, warriors and engines of war with which to set their foes ablaze. As such, there are many different ways to begin collecting an army of Thousand Sons. Presented below are two possible starting forces, each quite different from the other but both providing exciting and enjoyable opportunities.

The first of these forces represents a gathering of warriors who serve the Arch-Sorcerer of Tzeentch, Ahzek Ahriman. Ahriman himself commands this force, and he rides a Disc of Tzeentch to battle. Accompanying him is a squad of Rubric Marines led by an Aspiring Sorcerer. Five of the Rubric Marines have been given warpflamers to unleash torrents of death at close range, and one is equipped with a soulreaper cannon to provide devastating long-range firepower. Alongside this squad is a flock of braying Tzaangors. These avian mutants are armed with autopistols and chainswords, allowing them to swiftly mow through the enemy at close range. With one HQ choice and two Troops choices, this force can be taken as a Patrol Detachment. As the army is Battle-forged, it grants three Command Points that can be used to turn the tide of combat through the use of powerful Stratagems.

The second force is smaller, but far more elite. Magnus the Red leads this group, with a trio of Exalted Sorcerers from his Rehati serving as his battlefield cabal. Lastly, a squad of Scarab Occult Terminators serves as a bodyguard for the Daemon Primarch. With three HQ choices, one Elites choice and one Lord of War choice, this force constitutes a Supreme Command Detachment, providing one additional Command Point for a total of four.

This thrallband is known as Ahriman's Razor, and is an excellent base on which to build a larger force.

This cabal of powerful magi is called the Sons of the Cyclops, and is an alternative way to start marshalling Tzeentch's chosen Legion.

# THE FLAMES OF TIZCA

**Once you have the core of an army, more units can be added to create a truly imposing presence on the battlefield. Above is one such force, the Flames of Tizca – a terrifying conflux of warriors guided by both Magnus the Red and Ahriman.**

Standing at the front of the army is the Daemon Primarch of the Thousand Sons, Magnus the Red, his single eye gazing balefully at any foolish enough to face him. He has retained his Supreme Command Detachment – the Sons of the Cyclops – yet has deigned to allow Ahriman's forces to join his in battle, though for what purpose only Magnus and Ahriman know. To Magnus' left is his bodyguard of Scarab Occult Terminators, ready to eviscerate any lesser enemies that stand in their master's path. Also, following close behind him are three members of the Rehati – his cabal of Exalted Sorcerers. Though this trio act independently in battle, they also tend to remain close to each other, allowing them to share their collective power through the Cabalistic Focus Stratagem.

The other Detachment in this army is Ahriman's Razor, which the Arch-Sorcerer has grown into a full-blown Battalion Detachment. Ahriman on his Disc of Tzeentch shepherds the bulk of this Detachment along the right flank, with two squads of Rubric Marines, a squad of Scarab Occult Terminators and a flock each of Tzaangors and Tzaangor Enlightened creating a corona of destructive potential around him. A Chaos Rhino stands ready to transport the Rubric Marines or Tzaangors to where they are needed in battle, and a Tzaangor Shaman flies behind his bestial kin, filling their minds with his prophetic visions. Also on this flank, a Heldrake tears through the skies, its daemonic roar thundering through the air as its baleflamer ignites the ground.

In the rearguard of the army, another squad of Rubric Marines marches alongside a Sorcerer in Terminator Armour. These highly durable troops can be relied upon to secure and hold any backfield objective. Also at the rear is an Exalted Sorcerer on a Disc of Tzeentch who is holding back a Mutalith Vortex Beast, waiting for the right time to herd the unstable monstrosity into the enemy lines. In the vanguard is a squad of Scarab Occult Terminators equipped with a heavy warpflamer to make them truly ruinous at close range. And finally, following closely behind the elite infantry squad is a raging Helbrute, seeking to ameliorate its own agony by brutalising those unfortunate enough to be in its path.

For being a Battle-forged army, the Flames of Tizca starts with three Command Points. One more Command Point is added to this from the Sons of the Cyclops Supreme Command Detachment, and three Command Points are added from the Battalion Detachment Ahriman's Razor. This gives a grand total of seven Command Points.

1.  Magnus the Red

2.  Ahriman on Disc of Tzeentch

3.  Exalted Sorcerer on Disc of Tzeentch

4.  Sorcerer in Terminator Armour

5.  Exalted Sorcerers of the Rehati

6.  Scarab Occult Terminators with heavy warpflamer

7.  Scarab Occult Terminators with soulreaper cannon

8.  Scarab Occult Terminators with soulreaper cannon

9.  Rubric Marines

10. Rubric Marines

11. Rubric Marines

12. Chaos Rhino

13. Tzaangor Shaman

14. Tzaangor Enlightened with autopistols and chainswords

15. Tzaangors with autopistols and chainswords

16. Helbrute

17. Mutalith Vortex Beast

18. Heldrake

# WARRIORS OF LOST PROSPERO

This section contains all of the datasheets that you will need to fight battles with your Thousand Sons miniatures, and the rules for the weapons they can wield in battle. Each datasheet includes the characteristics profiles of the unit it describes, as well as any wargear and special abilities it may have. Any abilities that are common to several units are described below and referenced on the datasheets themselves.

## ABILITIES

The following ability is common to several **Thousand Sons** units.

### Death to the False Emperor

*The seething hatred that Chaos Space Marines harbour for the Corpse Emperor and his weakling Imperium is a weapon unto itself.*

Each time you make a hit roll of 6+ for a model with this ability in the Fight phase, it can, if it was targeting an **Imperium** unit, immediately make an extra attack against the same unit using the same weapon. These extra attacks cannot themselves generate any further attacks.

## DAEMONIC RITUAL

*Using dark pacts and blasphemous rituals, a champion of the Thousand Sons weakens the fabric of reality, creating a gateway to the warp through which Tzeentchian Daemons can pour.*

Instead of moving in their Movement phase, any **Thousand Sons Character** can, at the end of their Movement phase, attempt to summon a **Tzeentch Daemon** unit with this ability by performing a Daemonic Ritual (the character cannot do so if they arrived as reinforcements this turn).

Roll up to 3 dice – this is your summoning roll. You can summon to the battlefield one new **Tzeentch Daemon** unit that has the Daemonic Ritual ability and a Power Rating equal to or less than the total result. This unit is treated as reinforcements for your army and can be placed anywhere on the battlefield that is wholly within 12" of the character and is more than 9" from any enemy model. If the total rolled is insufficient to summon any unit, the ritual fails and no new unit is summoned.

If your summoning roll included any doubles, your character suffers a mortal wound. If it contained any triples, it instead suffers D3 mortal wounds.

*'They were less than nothing, yet I have rendered them immortal in the truest sense of the word. Who here can say they would choose debased and corrupted life over purity in unchanging death? Liars and fools tell us life is always precious, but we who have seen the spirit realm know this to be falsehood.'*

- *Ahzek Ahriman speaking to Magnus the Red*

# AHRIMAN

| NAME | M | WS | BS | S | T | W | A | Ld | Sv |
|------|---|----|----|---|---|---|---|-----|-----|
| Ahriman | 6" | 2+ | 2+ | 4 | 4 | 5 | 4 | 9 | 3+ |

Ahriman is a single model armed with the Black Staff of Ahriman, an inferno bolt pistol, frag grenades and krak grenades. Only one of this model may be included in your army.

| WEAPON | RANGE | TYPE | S | AP | D | ABILITIES |
|--------|-------|------|---|-----|---|-----------|
| **Ahriman** | | | | | | |
| Inferno bolt pistol | 12" | Pistol 1 | 4 | -2 | 1 | - |
| Black Staff of Ahriman | Melee | Melee | +2 | -1 | 3 | - |
| Frag grenade | 6" | Grenade D6 | 3 | 0 | 1 | - |
| Krak grenade | 6" | Grenade 1 | 6 | -1 | D3 | - |
| **Disc of Tzeentch** | | | | | | |
| Blades | Melee | Melee | 4 | 0 | 1 | After a model on this mount makes its close combat attacks, you can attack with its mount. Make 1 additional attack, using this weapon profile. |

| | |
|---|---|
| **WARGEAR OPTIONS** | • Ahriman may ride a Disc of Tzeentch (**Power Rating +2**). If he does so, he loses the **INFANTRY** keyword, gains the **DAEMON**, **CAVALRY** and **FLY** keywords, his Move characteristic is increased to 12" and his Disc will attack his enemies with its blades when he fights. |
| **ABILITIES** | **Death to the False Emperor** (pg 66)<br><br>**Arch-Sorcerer of Tzeentch:** You can add 1 to any Psychic tests or Deny the Witch tests you take for Ahriman.<br><br>**Sigil of Corruption:** Ahriman has a 4+ invulnerable save.<br><br>**Lord of the Thousand Sons:** You can re-roll hit rolls of 1 made for friendly **THOUSAND SONS** units within 6" of Ahriman. |
| **PSYKER** | Ahriman can attempt to manifest three psychic powers in each friendly Psychic phase, and attempt to deny three psychic powers in each enemy Psychic phase. He knows the *Smite* psychic power and three psychic powers from the Discipline of Change (pg 100) and/or Dark Hereticus discipline (pg 101). |
| **FACTION KEYWORDS** | **CHAOS, TZEENTCH, HERETIC ASTARTES, THOUSAND SONS** |
| **KEYWORDS** | **CHARACTER, INFANTRY, SORCERER, PSYKER, AHRIMAN** |

Of all those exiled from the Planet of the Sorcerers, none can raise a more potent army of mystics and warriors than Ahriman.

*Amidst the anarchy of battle, the Daemon Prince Esotephres sends a clarion call into the warp, summoning a throng of Pink Horrors who come loping into realspace.*

## DAEMON PRINCE OF TZEENTCH

**8 POWER**

| NAME | M | WS | BS | S | T | W | A | Ld | Sv |
|------|---|----|----|---|---|---|---|----|----|
| Daemon Prince of Tzeentch | 8" | 2+ | 2+ | 7 | 6 | 8 | 4 | 10 | 3+ |

A Daemon Prince of Tzeentch is a single model armed with a hellforged sword and a set of malefic talons.

| WEAPON | RANGE | TYPE | S | AP | D | ABILITIES |
|--------|-------|------|---|----|----|-----------|
| Daemonic axe | Melee | Melee | +1 | -3 | 3 | When attacking with this weapon, you must subtract 1 from the hit roll. |
| Hellforged sword | Melee | Melee | User | -2 | 3 | - |
| Malefic talons | Melee | Melee | User | -2 | 2 | Each time this model fights, it can make 1 additional attack with this weapon. A model armed with two sets of malefic talons can make 3 additional attacks with them instead. |

| **WARGEAR OPTIONS** | • This model may replace its hellforged sword with a daemonic axe or second set of malefic talons.<br>• This model may have wings (**Power Rating +1**). If it does, its Move characteristic is increased to 12" and it gains the **FLY** keyword. |
|---|---|
| **ABILITIES** | Death to the False Emperor (pg 66)<br><br>**Ephemeral Daemon:** This model has a 4+ invulnerable save.<br><br>**Prince of Tzeentch:** You can re-roll hit rolls of 1 made for friendly **THOUSAND SONS** and **TZEENTCH DAEMON** units within 6" of this model. |
| **PSYKER** | This model can attempt to manifest two psychic powers in each friendly Psychic phase, and attempt to deny one psychic power in each enemy Psychic phase. It knows the *Smite* psychic power and two psychic powers from the Discipline of Change (pg 100), Dark Hereticus discipline (pg 101) and/or Discipline of Tzeentch (pg 101). |
| **FACTION KEYWORDS** | **CHAOS, TZEENTCH, HERETIC ASTARTES, THOUSAND SONS** |
| **KEYWORDS** | **CHARACTER, MONSTER, DAEMON, DAEMON PRINCE** |

# EXALTED SORCERER

| NAME | M | WS | BS | S | T | W | A | Ld | Sv |
|---|---|---|---|---|---|---|---|---|---|
| Exalted Sorcerer | 6" | 2+ | 2+ | 4 | 4 | 5 | 4 | 9 | 3+ |

An Exalted Sorcerer is a single model armed with a force stave, an inferno bolt pistol, frag grenades and krak grenades.

| WEAPON | RANGE | TYPE | S | AP | D | ABILITIES |
|---|---|---|---|---|---|---|
| **Exalted Sorcerer** | | | | | | |
| Inferno bolt pistol | 12" | Pistol 1 | 4 | -2 | 1 | - |
| Plasma pistol | When attacking with this weapon, choose one of the profiles below. | | | | | |
| - Standard | 12" | Pistol 1 | 7 | -3 | 1 | - |
| - Supercharge | 12" | Pistol 1 | 8 | -3 | 2 | On a hit roll of 1, the bearer is slain. . |
| Warpflame pistol | 6" | Pistol D6 | 3 | -2 | 1 | This weapon automatically hits its target. |
| Force stave | Melee | Melee | +2 | -1 | D3 | - |
| Power sword | Melee | Melee | User | -3 | 1 | - |
| Frag grenade | 6" | Grenade D6 | 3 | 0 | 1 | - |
| Krak grenade | 6" | Grenade 1 | 6 | -1 | D3 | - |
| **Disc of Tzeentch** | | | | | | |
| Blades | Melee | Melee | 4 | 0 | 1 | After a model on this mount makes its close combat attacks, you can attack with its mount. Make 1 additional attack, using this weapon profile. |

| WARGEAR OPTIONS | • This model may replace its inferno bolt pistol with a plasma pistol or warpflame pistol. |
|---|---|
| | • This model may take a power sword. |
| | • This model may ride a Disc of Tzeentch (**Power Rating +1**). If he does so, he loses the **INFANTRY** keyword, gains the **DAEMON**, **CAVALRY** and **FLY** keywords, his Move characteristic is increased to 12" and his Disc will attack his enemies with its blades when he fights. |
| **ABILITIES** | **Death to the False Emperor** (pg 66) |
| | **Favour of Tzeentch:** This model has a 5+ invulnerable save. |
| | **Lord of the Thousand Sons:** You can re-roll hit rolls of 1 made for friendly **THOUSAND SONS** units within 6" of this model. |
| **PSYKER** | This model can attempt to manifest two psychic powers in each friendly Psychic phase, and attempt to deny one psychic power in each enemy Psychic phase. He knows the *Smite* psychic power and two psychic powers from the Discipline of Change (pg 100) and/or Dark Hereticus discipline (pg 101). |
| **FACTION KEYWORDS** | **CHAOS, TZEENTCH, HERETIC ASTARTES, THOUSAND SONS** |
| **KEYWORDS** | **CHARACTER, INFANTRY, SORCERER, PSYKER, EXALTED SORCERER** |

Profane chants ring loudly above the sound of inferno bolt fire as a cabal of Exalted Sorcerers weave their dread magic.

# SORCERER

| NAME | M | WS | BS | S | T | W | A | Ld | Sv |
|---|---|---|---|---|---|---|---|---|---|
| Sorcerer | 6" | 3+ | 3+ | 4 | 4 | 4 | 3 | 9 | 3+ |

A Sorcerer is a single model armed with a force sword, an inferno bolt pistol, frag grenades and krak grenades.

| WEAPON | RANGE | TYPE | S | AP | D | ABILITIES |
|---|---|---|---|---|---|---|
| Inferno bolt pistol | 12" | Pistol 1 | 4 | -2 | 1 | - |
| Plasma pistol | When attacking with this weapon, choose one of the profiles below. | | | | | |
| - Standard | 12" | Pistol 1 | 7 | -3 | 1 | - |
| - Supercharge | 12" | Pistol 1 | 8 | -3 | 2 | On a hit roll of 1, the bearer is slain. |
| Warpflame pistol | 6" | Pistol D6 | 3 | -2 | 1 | This weapon automatically hits its target. |
| Force stave | Melee | Melee | +2 | -1 | D3 | - |
| Force sword | Melee | Melee | User | -3 | D3 | - |
| Frag grenade | 6" | Grenade D6 | 3 | 0 | 1 | - |
| Krak grenade | 6" | Grenade 1 | 6 | -1 | D3 | - |

| WARGEAR OPTIONS | • This model may replace its inferno bolt pistol with a plasma pistol or warpflame pistol.<br>• This model may replace its force sword with a force stave. |
|---|---|
| ABILITIES | **Death to the False Emperor** (pg 66)<br><br>**Favour of Tzeentch:** This model has a 5+ invulnerable save. |
| PSYKER | This model can attempt to manifest two psychic powers in each friendly Psychic phase, and attempt to deny one psychic power in each enemy Psychic phase. It knows the *Smite* psychic power and two psychic powers from the Discipline of Change (pg 100) and/or Dark Hereticus discipline (pg 101). |
| FACTION KEYWORDS | **CHAOS, TZEENTCH, HERETIC ASTARTES, THOUSAND SONS** |
| KEYWORDS | **CHARACTER, INFANTRY, PSYKER, SORCERER** |

# SORCERER
## IN TERMINATOR ARMOUR

| NAME | M | WS | BS | S | T | W | A | Ld | Sv |
|---|---|---|---|---|---|---|---|---|---|
| Sorcerer in Terminator Armour | 5" | 3+ | 3+ | 4 | 4 | 5 | 3 | 9 | 2+ |

A Sorcerer in Terminator Armour is a single model armed with a force stave and inferno combi-bolter.

| WEAPON | RANGE | TYPE | S | AP | D | ABILITIES |
|---|---|---|---|---|---|---|
| Inferno combi-bolter | 24" | Rapid Fire 2 | 4 | -2 | 1 | - |
| Force stave | Melee | Melee | +2 | -1 | D3 | - |
| Power sword | Melee | Melee | User | -3 | 1 | - |

| WARGEAR OPTIONS | • This model may replace its inferno combi-bolter with a power sword.<br>• This model may take a Familiar. |
|---|---|
| ABILITIES | **Death to the False Emperor** (pg 66)<br><br>**Familiar:** If this model is accompanied by a Familiar, add 1 to the first Psychic test you take for him in each of your Psychic phases.<br><br>**Terminator Armour:** This model has a 5+ invulnerable save.<br><br>**Teleport Strike:** During deployment, you can set up this model in a teleportarium chamber instead of placing it on the battlefield. At the end of any of your Movement phases the model can use a teleport strike to arrive on the battlefield – set it up anywhere on the battlefield that is more than 9" away from any enemy models. |
| PSYKER | This model can attempt to manifest two psychic powers in each friendly Psychic phase, and attempt to deny one psychic power in each enemy Psychic phase. It knows the *Smite* psychic power and two psychic powers from the Discipline of Change (pg 100) and/or Dark Hereticus discipline (pg 101). |
| FACTION KEYWORDS | CHAOS, TZEENTCH, HERETIC ASTARTES, THOUSAND SONS |
| KEYWORDS | CHARACTER, INFANTRY, TERMINATOR, PSYKER, SORCERER |

A Terminator-armoured Sorcerer and his elite bodyguard advance upon the enemy with the inexorability of time itself.

# RUBRIC MARINES

| NAME | M | WS | BS | S | T | W | A | Ld | Sv |
|------|---|----|----|---|---|---|---|----|----|
| Rubric Marine | 5" | 3+ | 3+ | 4 | 4 | 1 | 1 | 7 | 3+ |
| Aspiring Sorcerer | 6" | 3+ | 3+ | 4 | 4 | 1 | 2 | 8 | 3+ |

This unit contains 1 Aspiring Sorcerer and 4 Rubric Marines. It can include up to 5 additional Rubric Marines (**Power Rating +7**), up to 10 additional Rubric Marines (**Power Rating +14**) or up to 15 additional Rubric Marines (**Power Rating +20**).
• Each Rubric Marine is armed with an inferno boltgun.
• The Aspiring Sorcerer is armed with a force stave and an inferno bolt pistol.

| WEAPON | RANGE | TYPE | S | AP | D | ABILITIES |
|--------|-------|------|---|----|----|-----------|
| Inferno bolt pistol | 12" | Pistol 1 | 4 | -2 | 1 | - |
| Inferno boltgun | 24" | Rapid Fire 1 | 4 | -2 | 1 | - |
| Plasma pistol | When attacking with this weapon, choose one of the profiles below. | | | | | |
| - Standard | 12" | Pistol 1 | 7 | -3 | 1 | - |
| - Supercharge | 12" | Pistol 1 | 8 | -3 | 2 | On a hit roll of 1, the bearer is slain. |
| Soulreaper cannon | 24" | Heavy 4 | 5 | -3 | 1 | - |
| Warpflame pistol | 6" | Pistol D6 | 3 | -2 | 1 | This weapon automatically hits its target. |
| Warpflamer | 8" | Assault D6 | 4 | -2 | 1 | This weapon automatically hits its target. |
| Force stave | Melee | Melee | +2 | -1 | D3 | - |

| WARGEAR OPTIONS | • The Aspiring Sorcerer may replace his inferno bolt pistol with a plasma pistol or warpflame pistol.<br>• Any Rubric Marine may replace his inferno boltgun with a warpflamer.<br>• For every ten models in the unit, one Rubric Marine may replace his inferno boltgun with a soulreaper cannon.<br>• One Rubric Marine may take an Icon of Flame. |
|---|---|
| ABILITIES | **Death to the False Emperor** (pg 66)<br><br>**All is Dust:** Add 1 to saving throws for Rubric Marines if the attack has a Damage characteristic of 1. In addition, the -1 modifier to hit rolls for moving and shooting with a Heavy weapon does not apply to Rubric Marines.<br><br>**Favoured of Tzeentch:** All models in this unit have a 5+ invulnerable save.<br><br>**Icon of Flame:** At the start of your Psychic phase, roll a D6 for each unit with an Icon of Flame. On a roll of 6 inflict 1 mortal wound on the closest enemy unit within 12" of the model carrying the Icon of Flame. |
| PSYKER | An Aspiring Sorcerer can attempt to manifest one psychic power in each friendly Psychic phase, and attempt to deny one psychic power in each enemy Psychic phase. He knows the *Smite* psychic power and one psychic power from the Discipline of Change (pg 100). When an Aspiring Sorcerer manifests the *Smite* psychic power, he inflicts 1 mortal wound instead of D3, or D3 mortal wounds instead of D6 if the Psychic test is more than 10. |
| FACTION KEYWORDS | **CHAOS, TZEENTCH, HERETIC ASTARTES, THOUSAND SONS** |
| KEYWORDS | **INFANTRY, PSYKER, RUBRIC MARINES** |

# TZAANGORS

| NAME | M | WS | BS | S | T | W | A | Ld | Sv |
|---|---|---|---|---|---|---|---|---|---|
| Tzaangor | 6" | 3+ | 4+ | 4 | 4 | 1 | 1 | 6 | 6+ |
| Twistbray | 6" | 3+ | 4+ | 4 | 4 | 1 | 2 | 7 | 6+ |

This unit contains 1 Twistbray and 9 Tzaangors. It can include up to 10 additional Tzaangors (**Power Rating +3**) or up to 20 additional Tzaangors (**Power Rating +6**). Each model is armed with Tzaangor blades.

| WEAPON | RANGE | TYPE | S | AP | D | ABILITIES |
|---|---|---|---|---|---|---|
| Autopistol | 12" | Pistol 1 | 3 | 0 | 1 | - |
| Chainsword | Melee | Melee | User | 0 | 1 | Each time the bearer fights, it can make 1 additional attack with this weapon. |
| Tzaangor blades | Melee | Melee | User | -1 | 1 | Each time the bearer fights, it can make 1 additional attack with this weapon. |

| WARGEAR OPTIONS | • Any model may replace its Tzaangor blades with an autopistol and chainsword.<br>• One Tzaangor can take a brayhorn. |
|---|---|
| ABILITIES | **Aura of Dark Glory:** All models in this unit have a 5+ invulnerable save.<br><br>**Brayhorn:** Add 1 to Advance and charge rolls for a unit that includes a brayhorn.<br><br>**Relic Hunters:** You can re-roll failed hit rolls in the Fight phase for this unit when targeting a **CHARACTER**. |
| FACTION KEYWORDS | **CHAOS, TZEENTCH, HERETIC ASTARTES, THOUSAND SONS** |
| KEYWORDS | **INFANTRY, TZAANGORS** |

# CHAOS CULTISTS

| NAME | M | WS | BS | S | T | W | A | Ld | Sv |
|---|---|---|---|---|---|---|---|---|---|
| Chaos Cultist | 6" | 4+ | 4+ | 3 | 3 | 1 | 1 | 5 | 6+ |
| Cultist Champion | 6" | 4+ | 4+ | 3 | 3 | 1 | 2 | 6 | 6+ |

This unit contains 1 Cultist Champion and 9 Chaos Cultists. It can include up to 10 additional Chaos Cultists (**Power Rating +3**), up to 20 additional Chaos Cultists (**Power Rating +6**) or up to 30 additional Chaos Cultists (**Power Rating +9**). Each model is armed with an autogun.

| WEAPON | RANGE | TYPE | S | AP | D | ABILITIES |
|---|---|---|---|---|---|---|
| Autogun | 24" | Rapid Fire 1 | 3 | 0 | 1 | - |
| Autopistol | 12" | Pistol 1 | 3 | 0 | 1 | - |
| Flamer | 8" | Assault D6 | 4 | 0 | 1 | This weapon automatically hits its target. |
| Heavy stubber | 36" | Heavy 3 | 4 | 0 | 1 | - |
| Shotgun | 12" | Assault 2 | 3 | 0 | 1 | If the target is within half range, add 1 to this weapon's Strength. |
| Brutal assault weapon | Melee | Melee | User | 0 | 1 | Each time the bearer fights, it can make 1 additional attack with this weapon. |

| WARGEAR OPTIONS | • Any Chaos Cultist may replace their autogun with an autopistol and brutal assault weapon.<br>• For every ten models in the unit, one Chaos Cultist may replace their autogun with a heavy stubber or a flamer.<br>• The Cultist Champion may replace their autogun with a shotgun or a brutal assault weapon and autopistol. |
|---|---|
| FACTION KEYWORDS | **CHAOS, TZEENTCH, HERETIC ASTARTES, THOUSAND SONS** |
| KEYWORDS | **INFANTRY, CHAOS CULTISTS** |

# HORRORS

**5 POWER**

| NAME | M | WS | BS | S | T | W | A | Ld | Sv |
|------|---|----|----|---|---|---|---|----|----|
| Pink Horror | 6" | 4+ | 4+ | 3 | 3 | 1 | 1 | 7 | 6+ |
| Blue Horror | 6" | 5+ | - | 2 | 3 | 1 | 1 | 7 | 6+ |
| Pair of Brimstone Horrors | 6" | 5+ | - | 1 | 3 | 1 | 2 | 7 | 6+ |

This unit contains 10 Pink, Blue or pairs of Brimstone Horrors, in any combination. It can include up to 10 additional Horrors (**Power Rating +5**) or up to 20 additional Horrors (**Power Rating +10**).
• Pink Horrors are armed with coruscating flames. Blue Horrors and Brimstone Horrors simply scrabble at anyone who comes too close.

| WEAPON | RANGE | TYPE | S | AP | D | ABILITIES |
|--------|-------|------|---|----|----|-----------|
| Coruscating flames | 18" | Assault 2 | User | 0 | 1 | - |

| WARGEAR OPTIONS | • For every ten models in the unit, one Pink Horror may take an Instrument of Chaos. |
|---|---|
| | • For every ten models in the unit, one Pink Horror may take a Daemonic Icon. |

| ABILITIES | **Daemonic Ritual** (pg 68) | **Split:** Each time a Pink Horror is slain, you can add up to two Blue Horrors to this unit before you remove the slain Pink Horror. Each time a Blue Horror is slain, you can add one pair of Brimstone Horrors to this unit before you remove the slain Blue Horror. The replacement models cannot be placed within 1" of an enemy model. Note that Horrors that flee do not generate any extra models for their unit. |
|---|---|---|
| | **Ephemeral Daemons:** Pink Horrors have a 4+ invulnerable save. Blue Horrors have a 5+ invulnerable save. Pairs of Brimstone Horrors have a 6+ invulnerable save. | |
| | **Iridescent Horror:** When you set up this unit for the first time, you may select a single Pink Horror in the unit – that model has an Attacks characteristic of 2, instead of 1. | *Matched Play: In matched play you must pay reinforcement points for each and every Blue and Brimstone Horror model that you add to a unit of Horrors, but the additional models can take the unit above its starting strength.* |
| | **Magic Made Manifest:** A unit of Horrors can attempt to manifest one psychic power in each friendly Psychic phase, and attempt to deny one psychic power in each enemy Psychic phase. However, when you do so, only roll a single D6 for the Psychic test or Deny the Witch test, and use the result of the single dice roll to determine the outcome. Note that this means that Horrors will never suffer Perils of the Warp. | **Daemonic Icon:** If you roll a 1 when taking a Morale test for a unit with any Daemonic Icons, no models flee and D6 slain Pink Horrors are instead added to the unit. |
| | | **Magical Horde:** Change the Type of this unit's coruscating flames to Assault 3 whilst the unit contains 20 or more Pink Horrors. |
| | **Instrument of Chaos:** A unit that includes any Instruments of Chaos adds 1 to their Advance and charge rolls. | |

| PSYKER | This unit can attempt to manifest one psychic power in each friendly Psychic phase, and attempt to deny one psychic power in each enemy Psychic phase. It knows the *Smite* power. When manifesting or denying a psychic power, first select a model in the unit – measure range, visibility etc. from this model. If a Brimstone Horror is selected, it is slain after the psychic power has been attempted and, if successful, resolved. |
|---|---|
| FACTION KEYWORDS | **CHAOS, TZEENTCH, DAEMON** |
| KEYWORDS | **INFANTRY, PSYKER, HORRORS** |

# TZAANGOR SHAMAN

**POWER 5**

| NAME | M | WS | BS | S | T | W | A | Ld | Sv |
|---|---|---|---|---|---|---|---|---|---|
| Tzaangor Shaman | 12" | 3+ | 3+ | 4 | 4 | 4 | 3 | 8 | 6+ |

A Tzaangor Shaman is a single model armed with a force stave. It rides to battle atop a Disc of Tzeentch, which attacks with its blades.

| WEAPON | RANGE | TYPE | S | AP | D | ABILITIES |
|---|---|---|---|---|---|---|
| **Tzaangor Shaman** | | | | | | |
| Force stave | Melee | Melee | +2 | -1 | D3 | - |
| **Disc of Tzeentch** | | | | | | |
| Blades | Melee | Melee | 4 | 0 | 1 | After a model on this mount makes its close combat attacks, you can attack with its mount. Make 1 additional attack, using this weapon profile. |

| ABILITIES | **Aura of Dark Glory:** This model has a 5+ invulnerable save. |
|---|---|
| | **Bestial Prophet:** Add 1 to any hit rolls you make for friendly **TZAANGOR** units within 6" of any Tzaangor Shaman models. |
| | **Sorcerous Elixir:** You can re-roll the first failed Psychic test you make for this model. This ability can only be used once per battle. |
| PSYKER | A Tzaangor Shaman can attempt to manifest one psychic power in each friendly Psychic phase, and attempt to deny one psychic power in each enemy Psychic phase. It knows the *Smite* psychic power and one psychic power from the Discipline of Change (pg 100). |
| FACTION KEYWORDS | **CHAOS, TZEENTCH, HERETIC ASTARTES, THOUSAND SONS** |
| KEYWORDS | **CHARACTER, CAVALRY, DAEMON, TZAANGOR, FLY, PSYKER, SHAMAN** |

# FLAMERS

**POWER 4**

| NAME | M | WS | BS | S | T | W | A | Ld | Sv |
|---|---|---|---|---|---|---|---|---|---|
| Flamer | 12" | 5+ | 3+ | 4 | 4 | 2 | 2 | 7 | 6+ |
| Pyrocaster | 12" | 5+ | 3+ | 4 | 4 | 2 | 3 | 7 | 6+ |

This unit contains 1 Pyrocaster and 2 Flamers. It can include up to 3 additional Flamers (**Power Rating +4**) or up to 6 additional Flamers (**Power Rating +8**). All models attack with flickering flames.

| WEAPON | RANGE | TYPE | S | AP | D | ABILITIES |
|---|---|---|---|---|---|---|
| Flickering flames | 12" | Pistol D6 | User | -1 | 1 | This weapon automatically hits its target. |

| ABILITIES | **Daemonic Ritual** (pg 68) |
|---|---|
| | **Ephemeral Daemons:** All models in this unit have a 4+ invulnerable save. |
| FACTION KEYWORDS | **CHAOS, TZEENTCH, DAEMON** |
| KEYWORDS | **INFANTRY, FLY, FLAMERS** |

# SCARAB OCCULT TERMINATORS

| NAME | M | WS | BS | S | T | W | A | Ld | Sv |
|---|---|---|---|---|---|---|---|---|---|
| Scarab Occult Terminator | 4" | 3+ | 3+ | 4 | 4 | 2 | 2 | 8 | 2+ |
| Scarab Occult Sorcerer | 5" | 3+ | 3+ | 4 | 4 | 2 | 2 | 9 | 2+ |

This unit contains 1 Scarab Occult Sorcerer and 4 Scarab Occult Terminators. It can include up to 5 additional Scarab Occult Terminators (**Power Rating +11**).
- Each Scarab Occult Terminator is armed with an inferno combi-bolter and a power sword.
- The Scarab Occult Sorcerer is armed with an inferno combi-bolter and a force stave.

| WEAPON | RANGE | TYPE | S | AP | D | ABILITIES |
|---|---|---|---|---|---|---|
| Heavy warpflamer | 8" | Heavy D6 | 5 | -2 | 1 | This weapon automatically hits its target. |
| Hellfyre missile rack | 24" | Heavy 2 | 8 | -2 | D3 | - |
| Inferno combi-bolter | 24" | Rapid Fire 2 | 4 | -2 | 1 | - |
| Soulreaper cannon | 24" | Heavy 4 | 5 | -3 | 1 | - |
| Force stave | Melee | Melee | +2 | -1 | D3 | - |
| Power sword | Melee | Melee | User | -3 | 1 | - |

| WARGEAR OPTIONS | |
|---|---|
| | • The Scarab Occult Sorcerer may replace his inferno combi-bolter with a power sword. |
| | • One Scarab Occult Terminator may replace his inferno combi-bolter with a heavy warpflamer or a soulreaper cannon. If the unit contains ten models, a second Scarab Occult Terminator may also do this. |
| | • One Scarab Occult Terminator may take a hellfyre missile rack. If the unit contains ten models, a second Scarab Occult Terminator may also do this. |

| ABILITIES | |
|---|---|
| | **Death to the False Emperor** (pg 66) |
| | **All is Dust:** Add 1 to saving throws for Scarab Occult Terminators if the attack has a Damage characteristic of 1. In addition, the -1 modifier to hit rolls for moving and shooting with a heavy weapon does not apply to Scarab Occult Terminators. |
| | **Terminator Armour:** All models in this unit have a 5+ invulnerable save. |
| | **Teleport Strike:** During deployment, you can set up this unit in a teleportarium chamber instead of placing it on the battlefield. At the end of any of your Movement phases the unit can use a teleport strike to arrive on the battlefield – set it up anywhere on the battlefield that is more than 9" away from any enemy models. |

| PSYKER | |
|---|---|
| | A Scarab Occult Sorcerer can attempt to manifest one psychic power in each friendly Psychic phase, and attempt to deny one psychic power in each enemy Psychic phase. He knows the *Smite* psychic power and one psychic power from the Discipline of Change (pg 100). When a Scarab Occult Sorcerer manifests the *Smite* psychic power, he inflicts 1 mortal wound instead of D3, or D3 mortal wounds instead of D6 if the Psychic test is more than 10. |

| FACTION KEYWORDS | CHAOS, TZEENTCH, HERETIC ASTARTES, THOUSAND SONS |
|---|---|
| KEYWORDS | INFANTRY, TERMINATOR, PSYKER, SCARAB OCCULT TERMINATORS |

The disincorporated warriors of the Scarab Occult march unharmed through salvo after salvo of Astra Militarum lasgun fire.

# HELBRUTE

| NAME | M | WS | BS | S | T | W | A | Ld | Sv |
|---|---|---|---|---|---|---|---|---|---|
| Helbrute | 8" | 3+ | 3+ | 6 | 7 | 8 | 4 | 8 | 3+ |

A Helbrute is a single model equipped with a multi-melta and a Helbrute fist.

| WEAPON | RANGE | TYPE | S | AP | D | ABILITIES |
|---|---|---|---|---|---|---|
| Combi-bolter | 24" | Rapid Fire 2 | 4 | 0 | 1 | - |
| Heavy flamer | 8" | Heavy D6 | 5 | -1 | 1 | This weapon automatically hits its target. |
| Helbrute plasma cannon | 36" | Heavy D3 | 8 | -3 | 2 | For each hit roll of 1, the Helbrute suffers a mortal wound after all of this weapon's shots have been resolved. |
| Missile launcher | When attacking with this weapon, choose one of the profiles below. | | | | | |
| - Frag missile | 48" | Heavy D6 | 4 | 0 | 1 | - |
| - Krak missile | 48" | Heavy 1 | 8 | -2 | D6 | - |
| Multi-melta | 24" | Heavy 1 | 8 | -4 | D6 | If the target is within half range of this weapon, roll two dice when inflicting damage with it and discard the lowest result. |
| Reaper autocannon | 36" | Heavy 4 | 7 | -1 | 1 | - |
| Twin heavy bolter | 36" | Heavy 6 | 5 | -1 | 1 | - |
| Twin lascannon | 48" | Heavy 2 | 9 | -3 | D6 | - |
| Helbrute fist | Melee | Melee | x2 | -3 | 3 | - |
| Helbrute hammer | Melee | Melee | x2 | -4 | D6 | When attacking with this weapon, you must subtract 1 from the hit roll. |
| Power scourge | Melee | Melee | +2 | -2 | 2 | Each time the bearer fights, it can make 3 additional attacks with this weapon. |

| WARGEAR OPTIONS | • This model may replace its multi-melta with a second Helbrute fist, or a twin heavy bolter, twin lascannon, Helbrute plasma cannon, or reaper autocannon.<br>• This model may replace one Helbrute fist with a missile launcher.<br>• This model may replace its Helbrute fist with a Helbrute hammer or power scourge.<br>• This model may incorporate a combi-bolter or heavy flamer into each Helbrute fist. |
|---|---|
| ABILITIES | **Crazed:** At the end of any phase in which this model loses any wounds, roll a D6. On a roll of 6, this model immediately makes a shooting attack as if it were your Shooting phase if there are no enemies within 1", or piles in and fights as if it were the Fight phase if there are enemies within 1". If there is no target visible to the model and within range, nothing happens.<br><br>**Battering Onslaught:** Add 1 to this model's Attacks characteristic if it is equipped with two melee weapons.<br><br>**Explodes:** If this model is reduced to 0 wounds, roll a D6 before removing the model from the battlefield; on a 6 it explodes, and each unit within 3" suffers D3 mortal wounds. |
| FACTION KEYWORDS | **CHAOS, TZEENTCH, HERETIC ASTARTES, THOUSAND SONS** |
| KEYWORDS | **VEHICLE, HELBRUTE** |

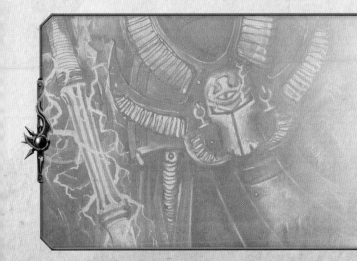

*'And what are the achievements of your fragile Imperium? It is a corpse rotting slowly from within while maggots writhe in its belly. It was built with the toil of heroes and giants, and now it is inhabited by frightened weaklings to whom the glories of those times are half-forgotten legends. I have forgotten nothing, and my wisdom has expanded far beyond mere mortal frailties.'*

*- Ahzek Ahriman*

# TZAANGOR ENLIGHTENED

| NAME | M | WS | BS | S | T | W | A | Ld | Sv |
|------|---|----|----|---|---|---|---|----|----|
| Enlightened | 12" | 3+ | 3+ | 4 | 4 | 2 | 2 | 7 | 6+ |
| Aviarch | 12" | 3+ | 3+ | 4 | 4 | 2 | 3 | 8 | 6+ |

This unit contains 1 Aviarch and 2 Enlightened. It can include up to 3 additional Enlightened (**Power Rating +2**) or up to 6 additional Enlightened (**Power Rating +4**). Each model is armed with a divining spear. They ride Discs of Tzeentch, which attack with their blades.

| WEAPON | RANGE | TYPE | S | AP | D | ABILITIES |
|--------|-------|------|---|----|----|-----------|
| **Tzaangor** | | | | | | |
| Autopistol | 12" | Pistol 1 | 3 | 0 | 1 | - |
| Fatecaster greatbow | 24" | Assault 2 | 5 | -1 | 1 | - |
| Chainsword | Melee | Melee | User | 0 | 1 | Each time the bearer fights, it can make 1 additional attack with this weapon. |
| Divining spear | Melee | Melee | +1 | -1 | 1 | The Damage of this weapon is increased to 2 on a turn in which the bearer charged. |
| **Disc of Tzeentch** | | | | | | |
| Blades | Melee | Melee | 4 | 0 | 1 | After a model on this mount makes its close combat attacks, you can attack with its mount. Make 1 additional attack, using this weapon profile. |
| **WARGEAR OPTIONS** | • All models in the unit may replace their divining spear with a chainsword and autopistol or a fatecaster greatbow. | | | | | | |
| **ABILITIES** | **Aura of Dark Glory:** All models in this unit have a 5+ invulnerable save. | | | | | | |
| | **Guided by Fate:** Each time you make a hit roll of 6+ for a model in this unit (except for the Disc's blades), do not make a wound roll for that attack – it is automatically successful. Saving throws may be attempted against these attacks as normal. | | | | | | |
| **FACTION KEYWORDS** | **CHAOS, TZEENTCH, HERETIC ASTARTES, THOUSAND SONS** | | | | | | |
| **KEYWORDS** | **CAVALRY, DAEMON, TZAANGOR, FLY, ENLIGHTENED** | | | | | | |

# SCREAMERS

| NAME | M | WS | BS | S | T | W | A | Ld | Sv |
|------|---|----|----|---|---|---|---|----|----|
| Screamer | 16" | 4+ | - | 4 | 4 | 2 | 3 | 7 | 6+ |

This unit contains 3 Screamers. It can include up to 3 additional Screamers (**Power Rating +4**) or up to 6 additional Screamers (**Power Rating +8**). Each model attacks with a lamprey bite.

| WEAPON | RANGE | TYPE | S | AP | D | ABILITIES |
|--------|-------|------|---|----|----|-----------|
| Lamprey bite | Melee | Melee | +2 | -3 | 2 | - |
| **ABILITIES** | **Daemonic Ritual** (pg 68) | | | | | | |
| | **Ephemeral Daemons:** All models in this unit have a 4+ invulnerable save. | | | | | | |
| | **Slashing Attack:** If this unit moves over any enemy units in its Movement phase (and it did not Fall Back), you can choose one of those enemy units and roll a D6 for each Screamer in this unit. Any rolls of 6 inflict a mortal wound on the enemy unit. | | | | | | |
| **FACTION KEYWORDS** | **CHAOS, TZEENTCH, DAEMON** | | | | | | |
| **KEYWORDS** | **BEAST, FLY, SCREAMERS** | | | | | | |

Wishing to see the creations of their god at work, a flock of Tzaangors herds three writhing Chaos Spawn towards the enemy lines.

# CHAOS SPAWN

| NAME | M | WS | BS | S | T | W | A | Ld | Sv |
|------|---|----|----|---|---|---|---|----|----|
| Chaos Spawn | 7" | 4+ | - | 5 | 5 | 4 | D6 | 9 | 5+ |

This unit contains 1 Chaos Spawn. It can include up to 4 additional Chaos Spawn (**Power Rating +2 per model**). Each Chaos Spawn attacks with hideous mutations.

| WEAPON | RANGE | TYPE | S | AP | D | ABILITIES |
|--------|-------|------|---|----|----|-----------|
| Hideous mutations | Melee | Melee | User | -2 | 2 | - |

| ABILITIES | |
|-----------|--|
| | **Fearsome:** Enemy units within 1" of any Chaos Spawn must subtract 1 from their Leadership. |

**Mutated Beyond Reason:** When a unit of Chaos Spawn makes its close combat attacks, roll a D3 and consult the table below:

| D3 | Result |
|----|--------|
| 1 | **Razor Claws:** The hideous mutations of all Chaos Spawn in the unit have an AP of -4 until the end of the Fight phase. |
| 2 | **Grasping Pseudopods:** Each Chaos Spawn in the unit adds 2 to its Attacks characteristic until the end of the Fight phase. |
| 3 | **Toxic Haemorrhage:** You can re-roll failed wound rolls for this unit until the end of the Fight phase. |

*Designer's Note: There are several abilities and psychic powers available to the Thousand Sons that can transform their victims into Chaos Spawn. If such an ability or psychic power instructs you to add a Chaos Spawn to your army, use this datasheet for the model. In a matched play game, you must pay reinforcement points in order to use any Chaos Spawn that are created. Each has a points value of 33 (this includes all of its weapons).*

| FACTION KEYWORDS | **CHAOS, TZEENTCH, HERETIC ASTARTES, THOUSAND SONS** |
|------------------|------------------------------------------------------|
| KEYWORDS | **BEAST, CHAOS SPAWN** |

## MUTALITH VORTEX BEAST

| NAME | M | WS | BS | S | T | W | A | Ld | Sv |
|---|---|---|---|---|---|---|---|---|---|
| Mutalith Vortex Beast | * | 4+ | 4+ | 7 | 7 | 14 | * | 7 | 4+ |

**DAMAGE**

Some of this model's characteristics change as it suffers damage, as shown below:

| REMAINING W | M | A | VORTEX POWER |
|---|---|---|---|
| 8-14+ | 8" | 4 | 2+ |
| 4-7 | 6" | 3 | 3+ |
| 1-3 | 4" | 2 | 4+ |

A Mutalith Vortex Beast is a single model which attacks with enormous claws and a betentacled maw.

| WEAPON | RANGE | TYPE | S | AP | D | ABILITIES |
|---|---|---|---|---|---|---|
| Betentacled maw | Melee | Melee | User | -1 | 1 | Make 3 hit rolls for each attack made with this weapon, instead of 1. |
| Enormous claws | Melee | Melee | User | -2 | 2 | - |

| ABILITIES | |
|---|---|
| | **Aura of Dark Glory:** This model has a 5+ invulnerable save. |
| | **Mutant Regeneration:** At the beginning of each of your turns, this model regains 1 lost wound. |
| | **Warp Vortex:** At the start of each of your Shooting phases, you may have this model attempt to use a single Mutalith Vortex Power of your choice from the table below. Alternatively, you may randomly determine the power by rolling a D6 and consulting the table below; if you do so, you may attempt a second randomly determined power immediately after resolving the first power. Each time this model attempts to use one of its powers, roll a D6 to see if it is successful. If the result is equal to or greater than the Vortex Power characteristic shown in its damage table resolve the power's effects, otherwise the attempt to use the power fails and nothing happens. |

| D6 | MUTALITH VORTEX POWER |
|---|---|
| 1 | **Warp Flare**<br>Each enemy unit within 9" of the Mutalith Vortex Beast immediately suffers a mortal wound. |
| 2 | **Chaotic Infusion**<br>Pick a **TZEENTCH** unit from your army within 9" of the Mutalith Vortex Beast; add 1 to that unit's Strength characteristic until the end of the turn. |
| 3 | **Temporal Flux**<br>Pick a **TZEENTCH** unit from your army within 9" of the Mutalith Vortex Beast; you can re-roll failed charge rolls for the unit this turn. If the unit is already within 1" of an enemy unit, they fight first in the Fight phase as if they had charged this turn. |
| 4 | **Ephemeral Touch**<br>Pick a **TZEENTCH** unit from your army within 9" of the Mutalith Vortex Beast; improve the AP of all melee weapons wielded by that unit by 1 until the end of turn (for example, a weapon with an AP of 0 would have an AP of -1 instead). |
| 5 | **Maelstrom of Madness**<br>Pick an enemy unit within 9". Reduce its Leadership characteristic by 1 until the end of the turn. This is cumulative with other uses of this power (to a maximum of -3). |
| 6 | **Beam of Unreality**<br>Roll 3 dice; for each roll of 4+, the closest enemy unit within 18" of the Mutalith Vortex Beast and visible to it immediately suffers a mortal wound. |

**Unstable Energies:** If this model has 7 or fewer wounds remaining at the start of your Shooting phase, the ranges of its Mutalith Vortex Powers are doubled; however, it will suffer a mortal wound if you roll a 1 when the model attempts to use a power.

**Warp Implosion:** If this model is reduced to 0 wounds, roll a D6 before removing the model from the battlefield; on a 6 those nearby are damaged by searing warpfire as the vortex collapses in on itself and each unit within 6" suffers D6 mortal wounds.

| FACTION KEYWORDS | **CHAOS, TZEENTCH, HERETIC ASTARTES, THOUSAND SONS** |
|---|---|
| KEYWORDS | **MONSTER, MUTALITH VORTEX BEAST** |

# CHAOS PREDATOR

| NAME | M | WS | BS | S | T | W | A | Ld | Sv |
|------|---|----|----|----|----|----|----|-----|-----|
| Chaos Predator | * | 6+ | * | 6 | 7 | 11 | * | 8 | 3+ |

A Chaos Predator is a single model equipped with a Predator autocannon.

## DAMAGE

Some of this model's characteristics change as it suffers damage, as shown below:

| REMAINING W | M | BS | A |
|-------------|-----|-----|-----|
| 6-11+ | 12" | 3+ | 3 |
| 3-5 | 6" | 4+ | D3 |
| 1-2 | 3" | 5+ | 1 |

| WEAPON | RANGE | TYPE | S | AP | D | ABILITIES |
|--------|-------|------|---|----|----|-----------|
| Combi-bolter | 24" | Rapid Fire 2 | 4 | 0 | 1 | - |
| Combi-flamer | When attacking with this weapon, choose one or both of the profiles below. If you choose both, subtract 1 from all hit rolls made for this weapon. | | | | | |
| - Boltgun | 24" | Rapid Fire 1 | 4 | 0 | 1 | - |
| - Flamer | 8" | Assault D6 | 4 | 0 | 1 | This weapon automatically hits its target. |
| Combi-melta | When attacking with this weapon, choose one or both of the profiles below. If you choose both, subtract 1 from all hit rolls made for this weapon. | | | | | |
| - Boltgun | 24" | Rapid Fire 1 | 4 | 0 | 1 | - |
| - Meltagun | 12" | Assault 1 | 8 | -4 | D6 | If the target is within half range of this weapon, roll two dice when inflicting damage with it and discard the lowest result. |
| Havoc launcher | 48" | Heavy D6 | 5 | 0 | 1 | - |
| Heavy bolter | 36" | Heavy 3 | 5 | -1 | 1 | - |
| Lascannon | 48" | Heavy 1 | 9 | -3 | D6 | - |
| Predator autocannon | 48" | Heavy 2D3 | 7 | -1 | 3 | - |
| Twin lascannon | 48" | Heavy 2 | 9 | -3 | D6 | - |

| WARGEAR OPTIONS | • This model may replace its Predator autocannon with a twin lascannon.<br>• This model may take two heavy bolters or two lascannons.<br>• This model may take a havoc launcher and/or a combi-bolter, combi-flamer or combi-melta. |
|-----------------|---|
| ABILITIES | **Smoke Launchers:** Once per game, instead of shooting any weapons in the Shooting phase, this model can use its smoke launchers; until your next Shooting phase your opponent must subtract 1 from all hit rolls for ranged weapons that target this vehicle.<br><br>**Explodes:** If this model is reduced to 0 wounds, roll a D6 before removing the model from the battlefield; on a 6 it explodes, and each unit within 6" suffers D3 mortal wounds. |
| FACTION KEYWORDS | **CHAOS, TZEENTCH, HERETIC ASTARTES, THOUSAND SONS** |
| KEYWORDS | **VEHICLE, CHAOS PREDATOR** |

# CHAOS VINDICATOR

**8** POWER

**DAMAGE**
Some of this model's characteristics change as it suffers damage, as shown below:

| REMAINING W | M | BS | A |
|---|---|---|---|
| 6-11+ | 10" | 3+ | 3 |
| 3-5 | 5" | 4+ | D3 |
| 1-2 | 3" | 5+ | 1 |

| NAME | M | WS | BS | S | T | W | A | Ld | Sv |
|---|---|---|---|---|---|---|---|---|---|
| Chaos Vindicator | * | 6+ | * | 6 | 8 | 11 | * | 8 | 3+ |

A Chaos Vindicator is a single model equipped with a demolisher cannon.

| WEAPON | RANGE | TYPE | S | AP | D | ABILITIES |
|---|---|---|---|---|---|---|
| Combi-bolter | 24" | Rapid Fire 2 | 4 | 0 | 1 | - |
| Combi-flamer | When attacking with this weapon, choose one or both of the profiles below. If you choose both, subtract 1 from all hit rolls made for this weapon. | | | | | |
| - Boltgun | 24" | Rapid Fire 1 | 4 | 0 | 1 | - |
| - Flamer | 8" | Assault D6 | 4 | 0 | 1 | This weapon automatically hits its target. |
| Combi-melta | When attacking with this weapon, choose one or both of the profiles below. If you choose both, subtract 1 from all hit rolls made for this weapon. | | | | | |
| - Boltgun | 24" | Rapid Fire 1 | 4 | 0 | 1 | - |
| - Meltagun | 12" | Assault 1 | 8 | -4 | D6 | If the target is within half range of this weapon, roll two dice when inflicting damage with it and discard the lowest result. |
| Demolisher cannon | 24" | Heavy D3 | 10 | -3 | D6 | When attacking units with 5 or more models, change this weapon's Type to Heavy D6. |
| Havoc launcher | 48" | Heavy D6 | 5 | 0 | 1 | - |

| WARGEAR OPTIONS | • This model may take a havoc launcher and/or a combi-bolter, combi-flamer or combi-melta. |
|---|---|
| ABILITIES | **Smoke Launchers:** Once per game, instead of shooting any weapons in the Shooting phase, this model can use its smoke launchers; until your next Shooting phase your opponent must subtract 1 from all hit rolls for ranged weapons that target this vehicle.<br><br>**Explodes:** If this model is reduced to 0 wounds, roll a D6 before removing the model from the battlefield; on a 6 it explodes, and each unit within 6" suffers D3 mortal wounds. |
| FACTION KEYWORDS | **CHAOS, TZEENTCH, HERETIC ASTARTES, THOUSAND SONS** |
| KEYWORDS | **VEHICLE, CHAOS VINDICATOR** |

'UNNATURAL LIGHTNING TORE DOWN FROM THE SKY, YET THE KANOSAPHIAN DEFENDERS REMAINED UNTOUCHED. A REFRACTORY FIELD ARCED FROM THE BASE OF THE MESA TO THE TALLEST SPIRE, REPELLING THE LEGION'S TEMPESTUOUS BOMBARDMENT. AHZEK AHRIMAN THEN SPOKE TO HIS WARRIORS.

"MY BROTHERS. WE HAD HOPED TO SHOW THESE RENEGADES THE EMPEROR'S MERCY. THEY HAVE REMAINED DEFIANT, AND NOW MUST BE BOWED."

AHRIMAN ORDERED HIS ARMOURED COLUMNS TO BE BROUGHT FORWARD, WHERE THEY FIRED UPON THE MACRO-STRUTS SUPPORTING THE MESA. ON THE THIRD DAY, THE LAST OF THE MILE-LONG STRUTS WAS DEMOLISHED. THE MESA COULD NO LONGER SUPPORT THE ENORMOUS BULK OF THE CITY, AND THE KANOSAPHIAN CAPITAL CAME CRASHING DOWN TO THE EARTH BELOW.'

*- From the works of Kallimakus the Remembrancer, Appendix 8E*

## CHAOS LAND RAIDER

**19** POWER

**DAMAGE**
Some of this model's characteristics change as it suffers damage, as shown below:

| REMAINING W | M | BS | A |
| --- | --- | --- | --- |
| 9-16+ | 10" | 3+ | 6 |
| 5-8 | 5" | 4+ | D6 |
| 1-4 | 3" | 5+ | 1 |

| NAME | M | WS | BS | S | T | W | A | Ld | Sv |
| --- | --- | --- | --- | --- | --- | --- | --- | --- | --- |
| Chaos Land Raider | * | 6+ | * | 8 | 8 | 16 | * | 9 | 2+ |

A Chaos Land Raider is a single model equipped with a twin heavy bolter and two twin lascannons.

| WEAPON | RANGE | TYPE | S | AP | D | ABILITIES |
| --- | --- | --- | --- | --- | --- | --- |
| Combi-bolter | 24" | Rapid Fire 2 | 4 | 0 | 1 | - |
| Combi-flamer | When attacking with this weapon, choose one or both of the profiles below. If you choose both, subtract 1 from all hit rolls made for this weapon. | | | | | |
| - Boltgun | 24" | Rapid Fire 1 | 4 | 0 | 1 | - |
| - Flamer | 8" | Assault D6 | 4 | 0 | 1 | This weapon automatically hits its target. |
| Combi-melta | When attacking with this weapon, choose one or both of the profiles below. If you choose both, subtract 1 from all hit rolls made for this weapon. | | | | | |
| - Boltgun | 24" | Rapid Fire 1 | 4 | 0 | 1 | - |
| - Meltagun | 12" | Assault 1 | 8 | -4 | D6 | If the target is within half range of this weapon, roll two dice when inflicting damage with it and discard the lowest result. |
| Havoc launcher | 48" | Heavy D6 | 5 | 0 | 1 | - |
| Twin heavy bolter | 36" | Heavy 6 | 5 | -1 | 1 | - |
| Twin lascannon | 48" | Heavy 2 | 9 | -3 | D6 | - |

| WARGEAR OPTIONS | • This model may take a havoc launcher and/or a combi-bolter, combi-flamer or combi-melta. |
| --- | --- |
| ABILITIES | **Smoke Launchers:** Once per game, instead of shooting any weapons in the Shooting phase, a Chaos Land Raider can use its Smoke Launchers; until your next Shooting phase your opponent must subtract 1 from all hit rolls for ranged weapons that target this vehicle. **Daemonic Machine Spirit:** Ignore the -1 to hit modifier for moving and shooting Heavy weapons for this model. **Explodes:** If this model is reduced to 0 wounds, roll a D6 before removing the model from the battlefield and before any embarked models disembark; on a 6 it explodes, and each unit within 6" suffers D6 mortal wounds. |
| TRANSPORT | This model can transport 10 **THOUSAND SONS INFANTRY** models (each **TERMINATOR** model takes up the space of two other models). |
| FACTION KEYWORDS | **CHAOS, TZEENTCH, HERETIC ASTARTES, THOUSAND SONS** |
| KEYWORDS | **VEHICLE, TRANSPORT, CHAOS LAND RAIDER** |

# DEFILER

| NAME | M | WS | BS | S | T | W | A | Ld | Sv |
|------|---|----|----|---|---|---|---|----|----|
| Defiler | * | 4+ | * | 8 | 7 | 14 | * | 8 | 3+ |

| REMAINING W | M | BS | A |
|-------------|---|----|----|
| 8-14+ | 8" | 4+ | 4 |
| 4-7 | 6" | 5+ | 3 |
| 1-3 | 4" | 5+ | 2 |

A Defiler is a single model equipped with a battle cannon, a reaper autocannon, a twin heavy flamer and Defiler claws.

| WEAPON | RANGE | TYPE | S | AP | D | ABILITIES |
|--------|-------|------|---|----|----|-----------|
| Battle cannon | 72" | Heavy D6 | 8 | -2 | D3 | - |
| Combi-bolter | 24" | Rapid Fire 2 | 4 | 0 | 1 | - |
| Combi-flamer | When attacking with this weapon, choose one or both of the profiles below. If you choose both, subtract 1 from all hit rolls made for this weapon. | | | | | |
| - Boltgun | 24" | Rapid Fire 1 | 4 | 0 | 1 | - |
| - Flamer | 8" | Assault D6 | 4 | 0 | 1 | This weapon automatically hits its target. |
| Combi-melta | When attacking with this weapon, choose one or both of the profiles below. If you choose both, subtract 1 from all hit rolls made for this weapon. | | | | | |
| - Boltgun | 24" | Rapid Fire 1 | 4 | 0 | 1 | - |
| - Meltagun | 12" | Assault 1 | 8 | -4 | D6 | If the target is within half range of this weapon, roll two dice when inflicting damage with it and discard the lowest result. |
| Havoc launcher | 48" | Heavy D6 | 5 | 0 | 1 | - |
| Reaper autocannon | 36" | Heavy 4 | 7 | -1 | 1 | - |
| Twin heavy bolter | 36" | Heavy 6 | 5 | -1 | 1 | - |
| Twin heavy flamer | 8" | Heavy 2D6 | 5 | -1 | 1 | This weapon automatically hits its target. |
| Twin lascannon | 48" | Heavy 2 | 9 | -3 | D6 | - |
| Defiler claws | Melee | Melee | x2 | -3 | D6 | - |
| Defiler scourge | Melee | Melee | +4 | -2 | 3 | Each time the bearer fights, it can make 3 additional attacks with this weapon. |

| WARGEAR OPTIONS | • This model may replace its twin heavy flamer with a havoc launcher or Defiler scourge.<br>• This model may replace its reaper autocannon with a twin heavy bolter or twin lascannon.<br>• This model may take a combi-bolter, combi-flamer or combi-melta. |
|-----------------|---|
| ABILITIES | **Daemonic:** This model has a 5+ invulnerable save.<br><br>**Infernal Regeneration:** At the beginning of each of your turns, this model heals one wound.<br><br>**Smoke Launchers:** Once per game, instead of shooting any weapons in the Shooting phase, this model can use its smoke launchers; until your next Shooting phase your opponent must subtract 1 from all hit rolls for ranged weapons that target this vehicle.<br><br>**Explodes:** If this model is reduced to 0 wounds, roll a D6 before removing it from the battlefield; on a 6 it explodes, and each unit within 6" suffers D3 mortal wounds. |
| FACTION KEYWORDS | **CHAOS, TZEENTCH, HERETIC ASTARTES, THOUSAND SONS** |
| KEYWORDS | **VEHICLE, DAEMON, DAEMON ENGINE, DEFILER** |

## FORGEFIEND

| NAME | M | WS | BS | S | T | W | A | Ld | Sv |
|------|---|----|----|---|---|---|---|----|----|
| Forgefiend | * | 4+ | * | 6 | 7 | 12 | * | 8 | 3+ |

**DAMAGE**

Some of this model's characteristics change as it suffers damage, as shown below:

| REMAINING W | M | BS | A |
|-------------|-----|----|---|
| 7-12+ | 8" | 4+ | 4 |
| 4-6 | 6" | 5+ | 3 |
| 1-3 | 4" | 6+ | 2 |

A Forgefiend is a single model equipped with two hades autocannons and Daemon jaws.

| WEAPON | RANGE | TYPE | S | AP | D | ABILITIES |
|--------|-------|------|---|----|----|-----------|
| Ectoplasma cannon | 24" | Heavy D3 | 7 | -3 | D3 | - |
| Hades autocannon | 36" | Heavy 4 | 8 | -1 | 2 | - |
| Daemon jaws | Melee | Melee | User | -1 | 2 | - |

| WARGEAR OPTIONS | • This model may replace both hades autocannons with ectoplasma cannons.<br>• This model may replace its Daemon jaws with an ectoplasma cannon. |
|---|---|

| ABILITIES | **Daemonic:** This model has a 5+ invulnerable save.<br><br>**Infernal Regeneration:** At the beginning of each of your turns, this model heals one wound.<br><br>**Explodes:** If this model is reduced to 0 wounds, roll a D6 before removing the model from the battlefield; on a 6 it explodes, and each unit within 6" suffers D3 mortal wounds. |
|---|---|

| FACTION KEYWORDS | CHAOS, TZEENTCH, HERETIC ASTARTES, THOUSAND SONS |
|---|---|

| KEYWORDS | VEHICLE, DAEMON, DAEMON ENGINE, FORGEFIEND |
|---|---|

## MAULERFIEND

| NAME | M | WS | BS | S | T | W | A | Ld | Sv |
|------|---|----|----|---|---|---|---|----|----|
| Maulerfiend | * | 4+ | 4+ | * | 7 | 12 | * | 8 | 3+ |

**DAMAGE**

Some of this model's characteristics change as it suffers damage, as shown below:

| REMAINING W | M | S | A |
|-------------|-----|---|---|
| 7-12+ | 10" | 6 | 4 |
| 4-6 | 8" | 5 | 3 |
| 1-3 | 6" | 4 | 2 |

A Maulerfiend is a single model equipped with Maulerfiend fists and two magma cutters.

| WEAPON | RANGE | TYPE | S | AP | D | ABILITIES |
|--------|-------|------|---|----|---|-----------|
| Magma cutter | 6" | Pistol 1 | 8 | -4 | 3 | - |
| Lasher tendrils | Melee | Melee | User | -2 | 2 | Each time the bearer fights, it can make 6 additional attacks with this weapon. |
| Maulerfiend fists | Melee | Melee | x2 | -3 | 3 | - |

| WARGEAR OPTIONS | • This model may replace both magma cutters with lasher tendrils. |
|---|---|

| ABILITIES | **Daemonic:** This model has a 5+ invulnerable save.<br><br>**Infernal Regeneration:** At the beginning of each of your turns, this model heals one wound.<br><br>**Explodes:** If this model is reduced to 0 wounds, roll a D6 before removing the model from the battlefield; on a 6 it explodes, and each unit within 6" suffers D3 mortal wounds. |
|---|---|

| FACTION KEYWORDS | CHAOS, TZEENTCH, HERETIC ASTARTES, THOUSAND SONS |
|---|---|

| KEYWORDS | VEHICLE, DAEMON, DAEMON ENGINE, MAULERFIEND |
|---|---|

# CHAOS RHINO

**DAMAGE**
Some of this model's characteristics change as it suffers damage, as shown below:

| REMAINING W | M | BS | A |
|---|---|---|---|
| 6-10+ | 12" | 3+ | 3 |
| 3-5 | 6" | 4+ | D3 |
| 1-2 | 3" | 5+ | 1 |

| NAME | M | WS | BS | S | T | W | A | Ld | Sv |
|---|---|---|---|---|---|---|---|---|---|
| Chaos Rhino | * | 6+ | * | 6 | 7 | 10 | * | 8 | 3+ |

A Chaos Rhino is a single model equipped with a combi-bolter.

| WEAPON | RANGE | TYPE | S | AP | D | ABILITIES |
|---|---|---|---|---|---|---|
| Combi-bolter | 24" | Rapid Fire 2 | 4 | 0 | 1 | - |
| Combi-flamer | When attacking with this weapon, choose one or both of the profiles below. If you choose both, subtract 1 from all hit rolls made for this weapon. | | | | | |
| - Boltgun | 24" | Rapid Fire 1 | 4 | 0 | 1 | - |
| - Flamer | 8" | Assault D6 | 4 | 0 | 1 | This weapon automatically hits its target. |
| Combi-melta | When attacking with this weapon, choose one or both of the profiles below. If you choose both, subtract 1 from all hit rolls made for this weapon. | | | | | |
| - Boltgun | 24" | Rapid Fire 1 | 4 | 0 | 1 | - |
| - Meltagun | 12" | Assault 1 | 8 | -4 | D6 | If the target is within half range of this weapon, roll two dice when inflicting damage with it and discard the lowest result. |
| Havoc launcher | 48" | Heavy D6 | 5 | 0 | 1 | - |

| WARGEAR OPTIONS | • This model may take a havoc launcher and/or a combi-bolter, combi-flamer or combi-melta. |
|---|---|
| ABILITIES | **Self-repair:** Roll a D6 at the start of each of your turns; on a 6, this model heals one wound. |
| | **Smoke Launchers:** Once per game, instead of shooting any weapons in the Shooting phase, this model can use its smoke launchers; until your next Shooting phase your opponent must subtract 1 from all hit rolls for ranged weapons that target this vehicle. |
| | **Explodes:** If this model is reduced to 0 wounds, roll a D6 before removing it from the battlefield and before any embarked models disembark; on a 6 it explodes, and each unit within 6" suffers D3 mortal wounds. |
| TRANSPORT | This model can transport 10 **Thousand Sons Infantry** models. It cannot transport **Terminators**. |
| FACTION KEYWORDS | **Chaos, Tzeentch, Heretic Astartes, Thousand Sons** |
| KEYWORDS | **Vehicle, Transport, Chaos Rhino** |

Having been transported to the front lines in the face of heavy incoming fire, a squad of Rubric Marines marches on foot beside their Chaos Rhino. Their vicious salvoes rake the enemy lines even as the dead are crushed beneath the vehicle's grinding tracks.

*Having sighted its huddled prey, a Heldrake swoops down from the smoke-blackened skies to ignite the battlefield with its baleflamer.*

## HELDRAKE

**10** POWER

| NAME | M | WS | BS | S | T | W | A | Ld | Sv |
|------|---|----|----|---|---|---|---|----|----|
| Heldrake | * | * | 4+ | 7 | 7 | 12 | * | 8 | 3+ |

A Heldrake is a single model equipped with a hades autocannon and Heldrake claws.

| WEAPON | RANGE | TYPE | S | AP | D | ABILITIES |
|--------|-------|------|---|----|----|-----------|
| Baleflamer | 18" | Assault D6 | 6 | -2 | 2 | This weapon automatically hits its target. |
| Hades autocannon | 36" | Heavy 4 | 8 | -1 | 2 | - |
| Heldrake claws | Melee | Melee | User | -1 | D3 | When attacking models that can **FLY**, you may add 1 to this weapon's hit roll. |

| WARGEAR OPTIONS | • This model may replace its hades autocannon with a baleflamer. |
|-----------------|------------------------------------------------------------------|

| ABILITIES | **Daemonic:** This model has a 5+ invulnerable save.<br><br>**Infernal Regeneration:** At the beginning of each of your turns, this model heals one wound.<br><br>**Crash and Burn:** If this model is reduced to 0 wounds, roll a D6 before removing the model from the battlefield; on a 6 it crashes in a fiery explosion and each unit within 6" suffers D3 mortal wounds. |
|-----------|---|

| FACTION KEYWORDS | CHAOS, TZEENTCH, HERETIC ASTARTES, THOUSAND SONS |
|------------------|--------------------------------------------------|

| KEYWORDS | VEHICLE, DAEMON, DAEMON ENGINE, FLY, HELDRAKE |
|----------|-----------------------------------------------|

### DAMAGE

Some of this model's characteristics change as it suffers damage, as shown below:

| REMAINING W | M | WS | A |
|-------------|----|----|---|
| 7-12+ | 30" | 3+ | 4 |
| 4-6 | 20" | 4+ | 3 |
| 1-3 | 10" | 5+ | 2 |

## MAGNUS THE RED

**23** POWER

| REMAINING W | M | A | PSYCHIC PHASE BONUS |
|---|---|---|---|
| 10-18+ | 16" | 7 | +2 |
| 5-9 | 14" | 6 | +1 |
| 1-4 | 12" | 5 | 0 |

| NAME | M | WS | BS | S | T | W | A | Ld | Sv |
|---|---|---|---|---|---|---|---|---|---|
| Magnus the Red | * | 2+ | 2+ | 8 | 7 | 18 | * | 10 | 3+ |

Magnus the Red is a single model armed with the Blade of Magnus. Only one of this model may be included in your army.

| WEAPON | RANGE | TYPE | S | AP | D | ABILITIES |
|---|---|---|---|---|---|---|
| The Blade of Magnus | Melee | Melee | x2 | -4 | 3 | If a **CHARACTER** is destroyed by this weapon, you can add a Chaos Spawn to your army. Set up the Chaos Spawn within 6" of Magnus and more than 1" from any enemy models. |

| ABILITIES | Death to the False Emperor (pg 66) |
|---|---|
| | **Crown of the Crimson King:** Magnus the Red has a 4+ invulnerable save. In addition, roll a D6 whenever Magnus suffers a mortal wound as a result of Perils of the Warp; on a roll of 2+, that wound is ignored. |
| | **Gaze of Magnus:** When Magnus the Red manifests the *Smite* power, he inflicts D6 mortal wounds instead of D3, or 2D6 mortal wounds instead of D6 if the result of the Psychic test is more than 11. |
| | **Primarch of the Thousand Sons:** You can re-roll hit rolls of 1, and any dice rolls of 1 that are made as part of a Psychic test, for friendly **THOUSAND SONS** units within 9" of Magnus the Red. |
| | **Unearthly Power:** Whenever Magnus the Red attempts to manifest or deny a psychic power, add the bonus shown in his damage table to his Psychic test or Deny the Witch test. |
| PSYKER | Magnus the Red can attempt to manifest three psychic powers in each friendly Psychic phase, and attempt to deny three psychic powers in each enemy Psychic phase. He knows the *Smite* psychic power and three psychic powers from the Discipline of Change (pg 100), Dark Hereticus discipline (pg 101) and/or Discipline of Tzeentch (pg 101). |
| FACTION KEYWORDS | **CHAOS, TZEENTCH, HERETIC ASTARTES, THOUSAND SONS** |
| KEYWORDS | **CHARACTER, MONSTER, DAEMON, PRIMARCH, FLY, PSYKER, MAGNUS THE RED** |

The Daemon Primarch Magnus the Red is a towering colossus, an avatar of Tzeentch who can bend reality itself to his whims.

As the Masque of the Midnight Sorrow pursues Ahriman out of the webway, the Arch-Sorcerer springs his trap. Ranks of Rubricae march through the glacial pass to surround the Harlequins, and the frozen moon quakes with the thunder of battle.

# ARMOURY OF TIZCA

Many of the weapons borne by the Thousand Sons are based upon Imperial design, though over many millennia they have been reshaped by sorcerous energies. Even the brutal implements wielded by Tzaangors and Cultists are engraved with the profane symbols of the Changer of Ways. The profiles for these weapons of war are detailed below.

## MELEE WEAPONS

| WEAPON | RANGE | TYPE | S | AP | D | ABILITIES |
|---|---|---|---|---|---|---|
| Betentacled maw | Melee | Melee | User | -1 | 1 | Make 3 hit rolls for each attack made with this weapon, instead of 1. |
| Black Staff of Ahriman | Melee | Melee | +2 | -1 | 3 | - |
| The Blade of Magnus | Melee | Melee | x2 | -4 | 3 | If a **CHARACTER** is destroyed by this weapon, you can add a Chaos Spawn to your army. Set up the Chaos Spawn within 6" of Magnus and more than 1" from any enemy models. |
| Brutal assault weapon | Melee | Melee | User | 0 | 1 | Each time the bearer fights, it can make 1 additional attack with this weapon. |
| Chainsword | Melee | Melee | User | 0 | 1 | Each time the bearer fights, it can make 1 additional attack with this weapon. |
| Daemon jaws | Melee | Melee | User | -1 | 2 | - |
| Daemonic axe | Melee | Melee | +1 | -3 | 3 | When attacking with this weapon, you must subtract 1 from the hit roll. |
| Defiler claws | Melee | Melee | x2 | -3 | D6 | - |
| Defiler scourge | Melee | Melee | +4 | -2 | 3 | Each time the bearer fights, it can make 3 additional attacks with this weapon. |
| Disc of Tzeentch's blades | Melee | Melee | 4 | 0 | 1 | After a model on this mount makes its close combat attacks, you can attack with its mount. Make 1 additional attack, using this weapon profile. |
| Divining spear | Melee | Melee | +1 | -1 | 1 | The Damage of this weapon is increased to 2 on a turn in which the bearer charged. |
| Enormous claws | Melee | Melee | User | -2 | 2 | - |
| Force stave | Melee | Melee | +2 | -1 | D3 | - |
| Force sword | Melee | Melee | User | -3 | D3 | - |
| Helbrute fist | Melee | Melee | x2 | -3 | 3 | - |
| Helbrute hammer | Melee | Melee | x2 | -4 | D6 | When attacking with this weapon, you must subtract 1 from the hit roll. |
| Heldrake claws | Melee | Melee | User | -1 | D3 | When attacking models that can **FLY**, you may add 1 to this weapon's hit roll. |
| Hellforged sword | Melee | Melee | User | -2 | 3 | - |
| Hideous mutations | Melee | Melee | User | -2 | 2 | - |
| Lamprey bite | Melee | Melee | +2 | -3 | 2 | - |
| Lasher tendrils | Melee | Melee | User | -2 | 2 | Each time the bearer fights, it can make 6 additional attacks with this weapon. |
| Malefic talons | Melee | Melee | User | -2 | 2 | Each time a model with malefic talons fights, it can make 1 additional attack with this weapon. A model armed with two sets of malefic talons can make 3 additional attacks with them instead. |
| Maulerfiend fists | Melee | Melee | x2 | -3 | 3 | - |
| Power scourge | Melee | Melee | +2 | -2 | 2 | Each time the bearer fights, it can make 3 additional attacks with this weapon. |
| Power sword | Melee | Melee | User | -3 | 1 | - |
| Tzaangor blades | Melee | Melee | User | -1 | 1 | Each time the bearer fights, it can make 1 additional attack with this weapon. |

## OTHER WARGEAR

| WARGEAR | ABILITIES |
|---|---|
| Brayhorn | Add 1 to Advance and charge rolls for a unit that includes a brayhorn. |
| Daemonic Icon | If you roll a 1 when taking a Morale test for a unit with any Daemonic Icons, reality blinks and the daemonic horde is bolstered. No models flee and D6 slain Pink Horrors are instead added to the unit. |
| Familiar | If a model is accompanied by a Familiar, add 1 to the first Psychic test you make for it in each of your Psychic phases. |
| Icon of Flame | At the start of your Psychic phase, roll a D6 for each unit with an Icon of Flame. On a roll of 6 inflict 1 mortal wound on the closest enemy unit within 12" of the model carrying the Icon of Flame. |
| Instrument of Chaos | A unit that includes any Instruments of Chaos adds 1 to their Advance and charge rolls. |

## RANGED WEAPONS

| WEAPON | RANGE | TYPE | S | AP | D | ABILITIES |
|---|---|---|---|---|---|---|
| Autogun | 24" | Rapid Fire 1 | 3 | 0 | 1 | - |
| Autopistol | 12" | Pistol 1 | 3 | 0 | 1 | - |
| Baleflamer | 18" | Assault D6 | 6 | -2 | 2 | This weapon automatically hits its target. |
| Battle cannon | 72" | Heavy D6 | 8 | -2 | D3 | |
| Combi-bolter | 24" | Rapid Fire 2 | 4 | 0 | 1 | - |
| Combi-flamer | | When attacking with this weapon, choose one or both of the profiles below. If you choose both, subtract 1 from all hit rolls made for this weapon. | | | | |
| - Boltgun | 24" | Rapid Fire 1 | 4 | 0 | 1 | - |
| - Flamer | 8" | Assault D6 | 4 | 0 | 1 | This weapon automatically hits its target. |
| Combi-melta | | When attacking with this weapon, choose one or both of the profiles below. If you choose both, subtract 1 from all hit rolls made for this weapon. | | | | |
| - Boltgun | 24" | Rapid Fire 1 | 4 | 0 | 1 | - |
| - Meltagun | 12" | Assault 1 | 8 | -4 | D6 | If the target is within half range of this weapon, roll two dice when inflicting damage with it and discard the lowest result. |
| Coruscating flames | 18" | Assault 2 | User | 0 | 1 | - |
| Demolisher cannon | 24" | Heavy D3 | 10 | -3 | D6 | When attacking units with 5 or more models, change this weapon's Type to Heavy D6. |
| Ectoplasma cannon | 24" | Heavy D3 | 7 | -3 | D3 | - |
| Fatecaster greatbow | 24" | Assault 2 | 5 | -1 | 1 | - |
| Flamer | 8" | Assault D6 | 4 | 0 | 1 | This weapon automatically hits its target. |
| Flickering flames | 12" | Pistol D6 | User | -1 | 1 | This weapon automatically hits its target. |
| Frag grenade | 6" | Grenade D6 | 3 | 0 | 1 | - |
| Hades autocannon | 36" | Heavy 4 | 8 | -1 | 2 | - |
| Havoc launcher | 48" | Heavy D6 | 5 | 0 | 1 | - |
| Heavy bolter | 36" | Heavy 3 | 5 | -1 | 1 | - |
| Heavy flamer | 8" | Heavy D6 | 5 | -1 | 1 | This weapon automatically hits its target. |
| Heavy stubber | 36" | Heavy 3 | 4 | 0 | 1 | - |
| Heavy warpflamer | 8" | Heavy D6 | 5 | -2 | 1 | This weapon automatically hits its target. |
| Helbrute plasma cannon | 36" | Heavy D3 | 8 | -3 | 2 | For each hit roll of 1, the Helbrute suffers a mortal wound after all of this weapon's shots have been resolved. |
| Hellfyre missile rack | 24" | Heavy 2 | 8 | -2 | D3 | - |
| Inferno bolt pistol | 12" | Pistol 1 | 4 | -2 | 1 | - |
| Inferno boltgun | 24" | Rapid Fire 1 | 4 | -2 | 1 | - |
| Inferno combi-bolter | 24" | Rapid Fire 2 | 4 | -2 | 1 | - |
| Krak grenade | 6" | Grenade 1 | 6 | -1 | D3 | - |
| Lascannon | 48" | Heavy 1 | 9 | -3 | D6 | - |
| Magma cutter | 6" | Pistol 1 | 8 | -4 | 3 | - |
| Missile launcher | | When attacking with this weapon, choose one of the profiles below. | | | | |
| - Frag missile | 48" | Heavy D6 | 4 | 0 | 1 | - |
| - Krak missile | 48" | Heavy 1 | 8 | -2 | D6 | - |
| Multi-melta | 24" | Heavy 1 | 8 | -4 | D6 | If the target is within half range of this weapon, roll two dice when inflicting damage with it and discard the lowest result. |
| Plasma pistol | | When attacking with this weapon, choose one of the profiles below. | | | | |
| - Standard | 12" | Pistol 1 | 7 | -3 | 1 | - |
| - Supercharge | 12" | Pistol 1 | 8 | -3 | 2 | On a hit roll of 1, the bearer is slain. |
| Predator autocannon | 48" | Heavy 2D3 | 7 | -1 | 3 | - |
| Reaper autocannon | 36" | Heavy 4 | 7 | -1 | 1 | - |
| Shotgun | 12" | Assault 2 | 3 | 0 | 1 | If the target is within half range, add 1 to this weapon's Strength. |
| Soulreaper cannon | 24" | Heavy 4 | 5 | -3 | 1 | - |
| Twin heavy bolter | 36" | Heavy 6 | 5 | -1 | 1 | - |
| Twin heavy flamer | 8" | Heavy 2D6 | 5 | -1 | 1 | This weapon automatically hits its target. |
| Twin lascannon | 48" | Heavy 2 | 9 | -3 | D6 | - |
| Warpflame pistol | 6" | Pistol D6 | 3 | -2 | 1 | This weapon automatically hits its target. |
| Warpflamer | 8" | Assault D6 | 4 | -2 | 1 | This weapon automatically hits its target. |

As the Daemon Primarch's army advances towards the Imperial gun line, the clouds ignite with psychic fire and eldritch energy rains down upon the battlefield. Amidst this maelstrom of violence, the thunderous voice of Magnus calling upon the warp rings clear.

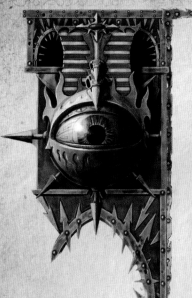

# SONS OF MAGNUS

In this section you'll find rules for Battle-forged armies that include THOUSAND SONS Detachments – that is, any Detachment which includes only THOUSAND SONS units. These rules include the abilities below and a series of Stratagems. This section also includes the Thousand Sons' unique Warlord Traits, Psychic Discipline, Relics and Tactical Objectives. Together, these rules reflect the character and fighting style of the Thousand Sons in your games of Warhammer 40,000.

## ABILITIES

If your army is Battle-forged, PSYKER units in THOUSAND SONS Detachments gain the Brotherhood of Sorcerers ability. In addition, Troops units in THOUSAND SONS Detachments gain the Disciples of Tzeentch ability.

## BROTHERHOOD OF SORCERERS

*When amassed on the field of battle, the Sorcerers of the Thousand Sons draw upon each other's psychic vigour, using the collective vortex of magical energy to augment their own spellcraft.*

The ranges of all psychic powers manifested by units with this ability are increased by 6".

## DISCIPLES OF TZEENTCH

*As they make their implacable march across the battlefield, the warriors of the Thousand Sons spread the corrupting influence of Tzeentch. The living amongst their ranks incant profane rituals, while the mere presence of the incorporeal serves as a grim tribute to the Changer of the Ways.*

A unit with this ability that is within range of an objective marker (as specified in the mission) controls the objective marker even if there are more enemy models within range of that objective marker. If an enemy unit within range of the same objective marker has a similar ability, then the objective marker is controlled by the player who has the most models within range of it as normal.

'The minds of gods are not for mortals to know, or to judge. Accept that Tzeentch has a place for all of us in his grand scheme, and be happy in the part you have to play. When his will is made manifest, you shall know, for the Imperium of my father shall be no more.'

*- Proclamation of Magnus the Red*

# WARLORD TRAITS

The Thousand Sons have ever been led into battle by the most psychically gifted of their number. Augmented further by the wisdom of ages and the dark power of Tzeentch, these sorcerers have each forged their own dark legend over the millennia.

If a **THOUSAND SONS CHARACTER** is your Warlord, he can generate a Warlord Trait from the following table instead of the one in the *Warhammer 40,000* rulebook. You can either roll on the table below to randomly generate a Warlord Trait, or you can select the one that best suits his temperament and preferred style of waging war.

## D6   RESULT

**1   ARROGANCE OF AEONS**

*The Warlord draws strength from a long-harboured hubris; the idea of submitting to the will of another is anathema to him.*

Re-roll failed Deny the Witch tests you take for this Warlord.

**2   UNDYING FORM**

*The Warlord's body has been transformed into psychocrystal, living granite or glittering cosmic dust, rendering it all but impervious to damage.*

Reduce all damage suffered by your Warlord by 1 (to a minimum of 1).

**3   AETHERSTRIDE**

*The Warlord has mastered the ability to fold time and space, enabling him to cross great distances with a single step and close upon his foes with terrifying speed.*

Your Warlord can Advance and charge in the same turn, and can re-roll failed charge rolls.

**4   LORD OF FORBIDDEN LORE**

*This Warlord has committed to memory many a grimoire and graven tome, giving him unparalleled knowledge of hexes, cantrips and destructive rites.*

Your Warlord knows one additional psychic power.

**5   OTHERWORLDLY PRESCIENCE**

*The Warlord has made countless pacts with denizens of the warp. These empyric entities whisper to him constantly, granting him visions of the twisting skeins of fate.*

Improve your Warlord's invulerable save by 1 (to a maximum of 3+).

**6   HIGH MAGISTER**

*This Warlord is a dark paragon within his sect, and by the raw might of his psyker's mind he is easily able to bend to his will the roiling powers of the warp.*

Add 1 to any Psychic tests you take for your Warlord.

'Free your mind in battle, and let the Architect of Fate guide you to new knowledge. If a manner of slaughter is unknown to you, will it into being. Reach through the warp into the inner parts of the living. Pull the bones from within their bodies and set their organs and tissues aflame. Bend their form to one more pleasing to Tzeentch and watch as they writhe in unknowing madness. These enemies believe they have faced true horror before; let us correct their staggering ignorance.'

- *Gilameht the Voracious, Daemon Prince of the Thousand Sons*

## NAMED CHARACTERS AND WARLORD TRAITS

The mightiest of the Thousand Sons are rightly feared for their fell power and sorcerous abilities on the battlefield. If one of the following named characters is your Warlord, they must be given the associated Warlord Trait shown below.

| NAMED CHARACTER | WARLORD TRAIT |
| --- | --- |
| Ahriman | Otherworldly Prescience |
| Magnus the Red | Lord of Forbidden Lore |

# STRATAGEMS

If your army is Battle-forged and includes any THOUSAND SONS Detachments (excluding Auxiliary Support Detachments), you have access to the Stratagems shown here, meaning you can spend Command Points to activate them. These help to reflect the unique tactics and strategies used by the Thousand Sons on the battlefield.

## LINEBREAKER BOMBARDMENT
**1CP**

*Thousand Sons Stratagem*

*The Chaos Space Marines learnt long ago that excessive force pays for itself in the terror that it causes.*

Use this Stratagem in your Shooting phase if a THOUSAND SONS Chaos Vindicator from your army is within 6" of 2 other friendly THOUSAND SONS Chaos Vindicators. The Vindicators cannot fire their demolisher cannons this phase: instead, select a point on the battlefield within 24" of all three vehicles and visible to them. Roll a D6 for each unit within 3" of that point. Add 1 to the result if the unit being rolled for has 10 or more models, but subtract 1 if the unit being rolled for is a CHARACTER. On a 4+, that unit suffers 3D3 mortal wounds.

## CORUSCATING BEAM
**3CP**

*Thousand Sons Stratagem*

*A sudden, lethal beam of magic is released from a Silver Tower.*

Use this Stratagem in the Shooting phase, if you have a THOUSAND SONS Warlord that did not move during your Movement phase. Instead of shooting with your Warlord's weapons, pick two points on the battlefield that are 9" apart and visible to him and draw an imaginary straight line 1mm wide between them. Roll a D6 for each unit that the centre of the line passes over, subtracting 1 from the result if the unit being rolled for is a CHARACTER. On a 4+, the unit being rolled for suffers D3 mortal wounds. You can only use this Stratagem once per battle.

## THE GREAT SORCERER
**1CP**

*Thousand Sons Stratagem*

*Those not driven mad by the worship of Tzeentch are given the power to harness the energies of the warp like no other.*

Use this Stratagem at the end of your Psychic phase. Select a THOUSAND SONS Psyker from your army. The psyker can immediately attempt to manifest one additional psychic power this turn.

## CABALISTIC FOCUS
**1CP**

*Thousand Sons Stratagem*

*Within a cabal, psychic energy is either shared or taken by force.*

Use this Stratagem before attempting to manifest a psychic power with a THOUSAND SONS Psyker from your army that is within 6" of at least 2 other friendly THOUSAND SONS Psykers. You can add 2 to the Psychic test.

## FIRE FRENZY
**1CP**

*Thousand Sons Stratagem*

*The unbridled wrath of a Helbrute is a useful tool in the hands of a commander who can direct it.*

Use this Stratagem in your Shooting phase, just before a THOUSAND SONS Helbrute from your army shoots. If that Helbrute did not move in its Movement phase, it can fire all of its weapons twice, but all of its attacks must target the nearest visible enemy unit.

## RELICS OF THE THOUSAND SONS
**1CP/3CP**

*Thousand Sons Stratagem*

*The halls of Tizca are replete with sorcerous esoterica.*

Use this Stratagem before the battle. Your army can have one extra Sorcerous Arcana for 1 CP, or two extra Sorcerous Arcana for 3 CPs. All of the Sorcerous Arcana that you include must be different and be given to different THOUSAND SONS CHARACTERS. You can only use this Stratagem once per battle.

## DAEMONFORGE
**1CP**

*Thousand Sons Stratagem*

*The Daemon Engines of the Chaos Space Marines are driven by a fathomless hatred born of the warp.*

Use this Stratagem in your Shooting or Fight phase when a THOUSAND SONS DAEMON VEHICLE is chosen to attack. Re-roll failed hit and wound rolls for that model until the end of the phase.

## KILLSHOT
**1CP**

*Thousand Sons Stratagem*

*The bloodthirsty Predator battle tanks of the Heretic Astartes hunt in packs to bring down especially large foes.*

Use this Stratagem in your Shooting phase if a THOUSAND SONS Chaos Predator from your army is within 6" of 2 other friendly THOUSAND SONS Chaos Predators. Add 1 to the wound and damage rolls for all of the Predators' attacks that target MONSTERS or VEHICLES this phase.

## BLASPHEMOUS MACHINES

**1CP**

### Thousand Sons Stratagem

*Heretic Astartes vehicles can be goaded to fury like wild beasts.*

Use this Stratagem before a **THOUSAND SONS VEHICLE** from your army attacks in the Shooting phase. Until the end of the phase, that vehicle can ignore the penalties for moving and firing Heavy weapons, or for Advancing and firing Assault weapons.

## WARPFLAME GARGOYLES

**1CP**

### Thousand Sons Stratagem

*On the hulls of vehicles swollen with the power of Tzeentch, gnashing maws open to spew fire on those nearby.*

Use this Stratagem at the start of any Fight phase. Pick a **THOUSAND SONS VEHICLE** from your army (but not a **HELBRUTE** or Heldrake) and roll a D6 for each unit (friend or foe) within 3" of it, subtracting 2 from the roll if the unit being rolled for is a **CHARACTER** or **VEHICLE**. On a 4+, the unit being rolled for suffers D3 mortal wounds.

## CHAOS FAMILIAR

**1CP**

### Thousand Sons Stratagem

*Though diminutive in stature, many lesser warp entities whisper dark secrets that can shift the tide of battle.*

Use this Stratagem at the start of your Psychic phase. Select a **THOUSAND SONS PSYKER** from your army. That model can replace a single psychic power with a power of your choice from the Dark Hereticus discipline (pg 101), Discipline of Change (pg 100) or Discipline of Tzeentch (pg 101).

## SORCEROUS PACT

**1CP**

### Thousand Sons Stratagem

*Guided by the will of Sorcerers, Daemons are enabled to stride freely into realspace.*

Use this Stratagem when a **THOUSAND SONS CHARACTER** attempts to summon a unit of **TZEENTCH DAEMONS** using a Daemonic Ritual. You can roll up to 4 dice rather than 3 for the summoning roll, and your character will not suffer any mortal wounds for rolling doubles or triples.

## VETERANS OF THE LONG WAR

**1CP**

### Thousand Sons Stratagem

*The hatred of the Traitor Legions has burned for millennia.*

Use this Stratagem when a **THOUSAND SONS INFANTRY** unit is selected to attack in a Shooting or Fight phase. Add 1 to all wound rolls made for the unit until the end of the phase.

## BOON OF TZEENTCH

**1CP**

### Thousand Sons Stratagem

*The path of Chaos can lead a Sorcerer to daemonhood, or it can see him transformed into a gibbering Chaos Spawn.*

You can use this Stratagem at the end of a Fight phase in which one of your **THOUSAND SONS CHARACTERS** (excluding **DAEMON CHARACTERS**) slays an enemy **CHARACTER**, **VEHICLE** or **MONSTER**. Roll 2D6 and look up the result below.

| 2D6 | Boon |
|-----|------|
| 2 | **Spawndom:** Your character is slain. However, before removing the model as a casualty, you can add a Chaos Spawn to your army. If you do so, set up the Chaos Spawn within 6" of the character before removing them. |
| 3 | **Arcane Occulum:** Add 6" to the Range of all of the character's shooting weapons. |
| 4 | **Temporal Distortion:** Add 3" to the character's Move characteristic. |
| 5 | **Prescient Foresight:** Each time the character loses a wound, roll a D6; on a 6, they do not lose that wound. If the character already has an ability with a similar effect, add 1 to any dice rolls you make for them to avoid losing wounds instead. |
| 6 | **Esoteric Insight:** Add 1 to any Psychic tests you take for the character. |
| 7 | **The Eye Opens:** Choose a boon of your choice (you cannot choose Spawndom or Daemonhood). |
| 8 | **Aura of Illusion:** Subtract 1 from hit rolls that target the character in the Fight phase. |
| 9 | **Aetherflame:** Add 1 to the Damage characteristic of the character's melee weapons. |
| 10 | **Crystalline Body:** Add 1 to the character's Toughness characteristic. |
| 11 | **Fragment of Immortality:** Add 1 to the character's Wounds characteristic. |
| 12 | **Daemonhood:** Your character is slain. However, before removing the model as a casualty, you can add a Daemon Prince of Tzeentch to your army. If you do so, set up the Daemon Prince within 6" of the character before removing them. |

Boons last for the rest of the battle. The same boon cannot be received by a model more than once – if this happens, choose a result the model has not yet received (excluding Spawndom and Daemonhood). In the unlikely event of a character accruing all of the available boons besides Spawndom and Daemonhood, roll a single D6 instead: on a roll of 1-3, they receive the Spawndom result; on a roll of 4-6, they receive the Daemonhood result.

Chaos Spawn or Daemon Princes of Tzeentch created by a boon must have the **TZEENTCH** keyword, and they do not cost any reinforcement points in a matched play game.

## WEBWAY INFILTRATION
### Thousand Sons Stratagem
**1CP/3CP**

*By traversing the wending paths of the webway, the Thousand Sons are able to outflank their foes.*

Use this Stratagem during deployment. If you spend 1 CP, you can set up one **Thousand Sons Infantry** unit from your army in the webway instead of placing it on the battlefield. If you spend 3 CPs, you can set up two such units in the webway instead. Any number of units in the webway can emerge at the end of any of your Movement phases – set each unit up anywhere on the battlefield that is more than 9" from any enemy models. You can only use this Stratagem once per battle.

## THE FLESH-CHANGE
### Thousand Sons Stratagem
**1CP**

*The flesh-change that afflicts the Thousand Sons has been embraced by most of the Legion's sorcerous brethren – some of whom Tzeentch rewards, others he punishes…*

Use this Stratagem at the start of any phase. Pick a **Thousand Sons Infantry Character** from your army. That character is slain, but you can add a Chaos Spawn to your army. If you do so, set up the Chaos Spawn within 6" of the character before removing them as a casualty. A Chaos Spawn created in this manner must have the **Tzeentch** keyword, and does not cost any reinforcement points in a matched play game.

## SOUL FLARE
### Thousand Sons Stratagem
**1CP**

*The power of Tzeentch courses through his flesh-and-blood servants, igniting their veins with warpfire. Upon death these servants may be given the honour of immolation as their body becomes a votive candle to their dark god.*

Use this Stratagem when a **Thousand Sons** Aspiring Sorcerer or Scarab Occult Sorcerer from your army is slain. Before removing that model as a casualty, roll a D6 for each enemy unit within 6" of that model, subtracting 2 from the roll if the unit being rolled for is a **Character** or **Vehicle**. On a 4+, the unit being rolled for suffers a mortal wound.

## INFERNO BOLTS
### Thousand Sons Stratagem
**1CP**

*Should the correct incantation be uttered, the bolt rounds of the Thousand Sons' battle tanks and Daemon Engines will flare into sorcerous life, burning through the armour of their prey with contemptuous ease.*

Use this Stratagem before the battle. Select a **Thousand Sons Vehicle** from your army and select a combi-bolter, combi-melta, combi-flamer, heavy bolter or twin heavy bolter that the model is equipped with. That weapon is upgraded to fire inferno bolt rounds. Change the AP characteristic of that weapon to -2 (only change the boltgun profile for a combi-melta or combi-flamer).

## FATED MUTATION
### Thousand Sons Stratagem
**1CP**

*Tzeentch often toys with the form of his minions, remoulding and mutating them into new shapes that he finds altogether more pleasing.*

Use this Stratagem in the Fight phase just before a unit of **Tzeentch** Chaos Spawn from your army fights. Instead of rolling a D3 for that unit's Mutated Beyond Reason ability this phase, you can choose the result from the table. In addition, you can re-roll the number of attacks each Chaos Spawn in the unit makes until the end of the phase.

## BALEFUL VORTEX
### Thousand Sons Stratagem
**1CP**

*The baleful vortexes surrounding Mutalith Vortex Beasts serve as conduits to the aether, through which the most malefic energies of the warp can be unleashed.*

Use this Stratagem after a Mutalith Vortex Beast from your army has resolved a Mutalith Vortex Power. Roll a D6 to randomly select a Mutalith Vortex Power. The Mutalith Vortex Beast immediately uses the power rolled, even if it has already used that power this phase. Furthermore, that power is automatically successful – no dice roll is necessary.

## VENGEANCE FOR PROSPERO
### Thousand Sons Stratagem
**1CP**

*The Thousand Sons have never forgiven the sons of Leman Russ for the destruction of their home world.*

Use this Stratagem just before a **Thousand Sons** unit from your army fights in the Fight phase. Until the end of the phase, that unit's Death to the False Emperor ability triggers on hit rolls of 4+ instead of 6+ for attacks that target a **Space Wolves** unit.

## CYCLE OF SLAUGHTER
### Thousand Sons Stratagem
**2CP**

*To the followers of Tzeentch, time is as mutable as flesh, enabling an orgy of slaughter to continue long after its natural conclusion.*

Use this Stratagem at the end of the Fight phase. Select a **Tzaangor** unit from your army – that unit can immediately fight an additional time.

# SORCEROUS ARCANA

The Thousand Sons have fought the Long War against the Imperium for ten millennia. Over the course of this war, many powerful artefacts have been found, forged or conjured into existence by the Sons of Magnus. Those relics most capable of channelling the Great Architect's powers are held in the screaming halls of Tizca, and carried to battle only when fate dictates.

If your army is led by a THOUSAND SONS Warlord, then before the battle you may give one of the following Sorcerous Arcana to a THOUSAND SONS CHARACTER. Named characters such as Ahriman already have one or more artefacts, and cannot be given any of the following arcana.

Note that some weapons replace one of the character's existing weapons. Where this is the case, you must, if you are playing a matched play game or are otherwise using points values, still pay the cost of the weapon that is being replaced. Write down any Sorcerous Arcana your characters may have on your army roster.

## SEER'S BANE

*The Seer's Bane is a Daemon weapon, quenched in the blood of a grand vizier and bound tight with a thousand curses. Its magic-infused alloys form the prison for the disgraced Lord of Change Malach'raccatax, who once uttered an unvarnished truth in the presence of Lord Tzeentch. It is said this ensorcelled weapon is the bane of learned men, and that it can cut through the minds of those that earn its master's ire as easily as it slices apart their flesh.*

Model with force sword or power sword only. Seer's Bane replaces the bearer's force sword or power sword and has the following profile:

| WEAPON | RANGE | TYPE | S | AP | D |
|---|---|---|---|---|---|
| Seer's Bane | Melee | Melee | User | -3 | D3 |

**Abilities:** The Strength of the bearer is doubled when targeting enemy PSYKER units or enemy units that include any models with a Leadership characteristic of 9 or higher with this weapon.

## DARK MATTER CRYSTAL

*By siphoning the perpetual gloom from the location where Mangel III once existed in realspace, a cabal of Sorcerers from the Cult of Magic created the Dark Matter Crystal. One in command of this powerful relic can use its energies to temporarily fold space, creating a localised wormhole through which he or his allies can step.*

Once per battle, at the end of your Movement phase, you can select the bearer or a friendly THOUSAND SONS INFANTRY unit within 12" of him. Remove that unit from the battlefield and immediately set it up anywhere on the battlefield that is more than 9" from any enemy models. This does not count as Falling Back if the unit was within 1" of any enemy models.

## HELM OF THE THIRD EYE

*Many of the Thousand Sons' disciplines teach of a mystical third eye that stares out from the forehead, seeing with far more than sight alone and even staring into the souls of men. This helm incorporates a crystalline eyeball that allows the wearer to perceive the intent of those around him, giving him a chance to react even before they have committed to their next action.*

If your army is Battle-forged and the wearer is on the battlefield, roll a D6 each time your opponent uses a Stratagem. On a 5+ you gain 1 Command Point.

## CORUSCATOR

*Of all the warp-forged weapons carried to battle by the Thousand Sons, Coruscator is the most revered. Since the time of the Horus Heresy, it has taken the lives of countless loyalist Space Marines, and its daemonic spirit will take any chance to stoke the fires of hatred that eat away at the Imperium from within.*

Model with inferno bolt pistol only. Coruscator replaces the bearer's inferno bolt pistol and has the following profile:

| WEAPON | RANGE | TYPE | S | AP | D |
|---|---|---|---|---|---|
| Coruscator | 12" | Pistol 3 | 4 | -2 | D3 |

## ATHENAEAN SCROLLS

*Ahriman consumed the knowledge contained in the Athenaeum of Kallimakus long ago. However, not all of the Athenaeum's founders were slain when their repository of knowledge was destroyed. Some of their Apollonian disciplines have since been transcribed on sanctified papyrus in order to keep an echo of that great library in existence. One who possesses the so-called 'Athenaean Scrolls' has access to advanced psychic techniques that make his spells all but unstoppable.*

If you roll a double when making a successful Psychic test for the bearer, your opponent cannot attempt to resist that psychic power with a Deny the Witch test or negate it by any means. Note that the psyker will still suffer Perils of the Warp on a roll of double 1 or double 6, and if slain by Perils of the Warp, the power they were trying to manifest will still automatically fail.

## THE PRISMATIC STAFF

*This long-hafted weapon is bound with hypnotic rune-forms, and by intoning the command words its wielder can create multiple illusory duplicates of themselves to confuse their enemies. When the Long War erupts on a battlefield, the misdirection bought by the staff's magic can be the difference between life and death.*

Model with force stave only. The Prismatic Staff replaces the bearer's force stave and has the following profile:

| WEAPON | RANGE | TYPE | S | AP | D |
|---|---|---|---|---|---|
| The Prismatic Staff | Melee | Melee | +2 | -1 | D3 |

**Abilities:** The bearer can shoot and charge during a turn in which it Fell Back.

# PSYCHIC POWERS

There are few in the galaxy whose mastery of warp energies is more extensive than the Sorcerers of the Thousand Sons. Through profane rituals and blasphemous incantations these energies are released upon their enemies and Tzeentch's will is made manifest.

Before the battle, generate the psychic powers for **Psykers** that can use powers from the Change, Dark Hereticus or Tzeentch disciplines using the following tables. You can either roll a D6 to generate their powers randomly (re-roll any duplicate results), or you can select the psychic powers you wish the psyker to have.

## DISCIPLINE OF CHANGE

| D6 | RESULT |
|----|--------|
| 1 | **Tzeentch's Firestorm:** *The psyker conjures a storm of pink and blue fire that mutates his foes, leaving capering Daemons that claw and bite in its wake.* <br> *Tzeentch's Firestorm* has a warp charge value of 7. If manifested, select an enemy unit that is within 18" of the psyker and visible to him. Roll 9 dice; the enemy unit you selected suffers a mortal wound for each roll of a 6. |
| 2 | **Boon of Mutation:** *The psyker channels the warping power of Chaos into a warrior marked for glory, transforming the champion until his flesh wrenches and flows.* <br> *Boon of Mutation* has a warp charge value of 7. If manifested, select a friendly **Thousand Sons Character** (but not a **Daemon Character**) within 3" of the psyker. Roll 2D6 and consult the chart on the Boon of Tzeentch Stratagem (pg 97) to see what effect this power has on that character for the rest of the game. |
| 3 | **Glamour of Tzeentch:** *The psyker twists and obscures the perceptions of his foes to the point that his allies become all but invisible.* <br> *Glamour of Tzeentch* has a warp charge value of 7. If manifested, select a friendly **Thousand Sons** unit within 12" of the psyker. Until the start of your next Psychic phase, your opponent must subtract 1 from any hit rolls they make for models that target that unit. |
| 4 | **Doombolt:** *The psyker hurls a bolt of roiling energy that blasts its targets into terrifying new shapes.* <br> *Doombolt* has a warp charge value of 9. If manifested, select an enemy unit that is within 18" of the psyker and visible to him; that unit suffers D3 mortal wounds and in their following Movement phase must halve their Move characteristic and cannot Advance. |
| 5 | **Temporal Manipulation:** *By creating a pocket of dilated time around an injured ally, the psyker drastically accelerates the rate at which wounds heal and muscles regrow.* <br> *Temporal Manipulation* has a warp charge value of 6. If manifested, select a friendly **Thousand Sons** model within 12" of the psyker. That model immediately heals D3 wounds. |
| 6 | **Weaver of Fates:** *The psyker traces the skeins of the future to see the fates of battle. Forewarned of imminent danger, warriors dodge bullets and sword blows with seemingly supernatural reflexes.* <br> *Weaver of Fates* has a warp charge value of 6. If manifested, select a **Thousand Sons** unit within 18" of the psyker. Until the start of your next Psychic phase, the invulnerable save of that unit is improved by 1 (to a maximum of 3+). Models that do not have an invulnerable save instead gain a 5+ invulnerable save. |

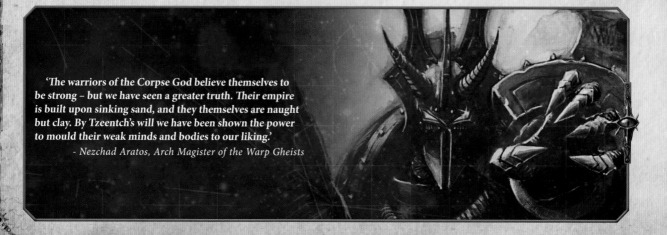

'The warriors of the Corpse God believe themselves to be strong – but we have seen a greater truth. Their empire is built upon sinking sand, and they themselves are naught but clay. By Tzeentch's will we have been shown the power to mould their weak minds and bodies to our liking.'

- Nezchad Aratos, Arch Magister of the Warp Gheists

# Dark Hereticus Discipline

| D6 | RESULT |
|----|--------|
| 1 | **Infernal Gaze:** *Unholy power streams from the psyker's eyes, charring and melting everything caught in its path.* <br> *Infernal Gaze* has a warp charge value of 5. If manifested, select an enemy unit that is within 18" of the psyker and visible to him and roll 3 dice. The target suffers one mortal wound for each roll of 4+. |
| 2 | **Death Hex:** *The Sorcerer places a dire hex upon his enemies. Wards and energised shields flicker and fail, leaving the foe exposed.* <br> *Death Hex* has a warp charge value of 8. If manifested, select an enemy unit that is within 12" of the psyker and visible to him. Until the start of your next Psychic phase, that unit cannot take invulnerable saves. |
| 3 | **Gift of Chaos:** *As the power of the warp surges through the psyker's victim, bones snap and flesh rips as a new form takes shape.* <br> *Gift of Chaos* has a warp charge value of 6. If manifested, select an enemy unit that is within 6" of the psyker and visible to him and roll a D6. If the result is greater than the target's Toughness, it suffers D3+3 mortal wounds. If a **Character** is slain by this power, you can add a Chaos Spawn to your army and set it up within 1" of the character before it is removed. |
| 4 | **Prescience:** *By focusing his warp-sight the psyker can guide the aim of his allies, bringing a swift and merciless death to their foes.* <br> *Prescience* has a warp charge value of 7. If manifested, select a **Heretic Astartes** unit within 18" of the psyker. You can add 1 to all hit rolls made for that unit until the start of your next Psychic phase. |
| 5 | **Diabolic Strength:** *The unholy energies of Chaos course through the recipient, swelling his frame with the strength to tear a tank in two.* <br> *Diabolic Strength* has a warp charge value of 6. If manifested, select a **Heretic Astartes** model within 12" of the psyker. Until the start of your next Psychic phase, add 2 to that model's Strength characteristic and 1 to its Attacks characteristic. |
| 6 | **Warptime:** *The power of the immaterium bursts from the psyker, warping time and heightening the speed of his allies.* <br> *Warptime* has a warp charge value of 6. If manifested, pick a **Heretic Astartes** unit within 3" of the psyker. That unit can immediately move as if it were its Movement phase. You cannot use *Warptime* on a unit more than once per Psychic phase. |

# Discipline of Tzeentch

| D6 | RESULT |
|----|--------|
| 1 | **Boon of Change:** *As the Daemon chants, their minions begin to twist and new forms take shape as the will of Tzeentch demands.* <br> *Boon of Change* has a warp charge value of 7. If manifested, select a friendly **Tzeentch Daemon** unit within 18" of the psyker and roll a D3. Consult the table below to discover what characteristic bonus all models in that unit receive until the start of your next Psychic phase. <br><br> **D3 EFFECT** <br> 1 Extra Limb: +1 Attack <br> 2 Mystic Strength: +1 Strength <br> 3 Iron Skin: +1 Toughness |
| 2 | **Bolt of Change:** *The Daemon unleashes a bolt of roiling warp energy that wracks the foe with sickening and uncontrollable mutations.* <br> *Bolt of Change* has a warp charge value of 9. If manifested, select an enemy unit that is within 18" of the psyker and visible to him. That unit suffers D3 mortal wounds. If a **Character** is slain by this psychic power, you can add a Chaos Spawn to your army, and set it up within 1" of the character before it is removed. |
| 3 | **Gaze of Fate:** *The Daemon uses his powers of precognition to unravel the strands of destiny, and in doing so discovers the one true path to victory.* <br> *Gaze of Fate* has a warp charge value of 6. If manifested, you can re-roll a single dice roll later during your turn. |
| 4 | **Treason of Tzeentch:** *The psyker reaches his thoughts into the minds of his victims, subverting their will and turning them upon their own allies.* <br> *Treason of Tzeentch* has a warp charge value of 8. If manifested, select an enemy **Character** that is within 18" of the psyker and visible to him (excluding the opponent's Warlord) and roll 2D6. If the result is greater than the character's Leadership, you can treat the model as if it were a friendly model in your army in your Shooting, Charge and Fight phases. At the end of the Fight phase, the character reverts to being an enemy model. |
| 5 | **Flickering Flames:** *Cackling madly, the psyker's minions are wreathed in pink and blue flames that leap forth to consume their foes.* <br> *Flickering Flames* has a warp charge value of 5. If manifested, pick a friendly **Tzeentch Daemon** unit within 18" of the psyker. Until your next Psychic phase, add 1 to any wound rolls made for that unit's shooting weapons. |
| 6 | **Infernal Gateway:** *The psyker opens a portal to the warp, a tear in the fabric of the mortal plane that sucks foes into certain oblivion.* <br> *Infernal Gateway* has a warp charge value of 8. If manifested, identify the nearest enemy model that is within 12" of the psyker and visible to him; that model's unit, and every other unit (friend or foe) within 3" of that model, suffers D3 mortal wounds. The number of mortal wounds inflicted is D6 instead if the power is manifested with a Psychic test of 12+. |

# POINTS VALUES

If you are playing a matched play game, or a game that uses a points limit, you can use the following lists to determine the total points cost of your army. Simply add together the points costs of all your models and the wargear they are equipped with to determine your army's total points value.

## HQ

| UNIT | MODELS PER UNIT | POINTS PER MODEL (Does not include wargear) |
|---|---|---|
| Daemon Prince of Tzeentch | 1 | 146 |
| Daemon Prince of Tzeentch with Wings | 1 | 170 |
| Exalted Sorcerer | 1 | 112 |
| Exalted Sorcerer on Disc of Tzeentch | 1 | 132 |
| Sorcerer | 1 | 95 |
| Sorcerer in Terminator Armour | 1 | 120 |

## TROOPS

| UNIT | MODELS PER UNIT | POINTS PER MODEL (Does not include wargear) |
|---|---|---|
| Chaos Cultists | 10-40 | 4 |
| Rubric Marines | 5-20 | 18 |
| Tzaangors | 10-30 | 7 |

## ELITES

| UNIT | MODELS PER UNIT | POINTS PER MODEL (Does not include wargear) |
|---|---|---|
| Helbrute | 1 | 72 |
| Scarab Occult Terminators | 5-10 | 33 |
| Tzaangor Shaman | 1 | 82 |

## FAST ATTACK

| UNIT | MODELS PER UNIT | POINTS PER MODEL (Does not include wargear) |
|---|---|---|
| Chaos Spawn | 1-5 | 33 |
| Tzaangor Enlightened | 3-9 | 15 |

## HEAVY SUPPORT

| UNIT | MODELS PER UNIT | POINTS PER MODEL (Does not include wargear) |
|---|---|---|
| Chaos Land Raider | 1 | 239 |
| Chaos Predator | 1 | 90 |
| Chaos Vindicator | 1 | 125 |
| Defiler | 1 | 140 |
| Forgefiend | 1 | 119 |
| Maulerfiend | 1 | 140 |
| Mutalith Vortex Beast | 1 | 150 |

## DEDICATED TRANSPORT

| UNIT | MODELS PER UNIT | POINTS PER MODEL (Does not include wargear) |
|---|---|---|
| Chaos Rhino | 1 | 70 |

## FLYER

| UNIT | MODELS PER UNIT | POINTS PER MODEL (Does not include wargear) |
|---|---|---|
| Heldrake | 1 | 138 |

## DAEMONS

| UNIT | MODELS PER UNIT | POINTS PER MODEL (Including wargear) |
|---|---|---|
| Flamers | 3-9 | 28 |
| Horrors | 10-30 | |
| - Blue Horrors | | 5 |
| - Pairs of Brimstone Horrors | | 3 |
| - Pink Horrors | | 7 |
| Screamers | 3-9 | 31 |

## NAMED CHARACTERS

| UNIT | MODELS PER UNIT | POINTS PER MODEL (Including wargear) |
|---|---|---|
| Ahriman | 1 | 131 |
| Ahriman on Disc of Tzeentch | 1 | 166 |
| Magnus the Red | 1 | 445 |

## RANGED WEAPONS

| WEAPON | POINTS PER WEAPON |
|---|---|
| Autogun | 0 |
| Autopistol | 0 |
| Baleflamer | 30 |
| Battle cannon | 0 |
| Combi-bolter | 2 |
| Combi-flamer | 11 |
| Combi-melta | 19 |
| Demolisher cannon | 0 |
| Ectoplasma cannon | 26 |
| Fatecaster greatbow | 2 |
| Flamer | 9 |
| Frag grenades | 0 |
| Hades autocannon | 25 |
| Havoc launcher | 11 |
| Heavy bolter | 10 |
| Heavy flamer | 17 |
| Heavy stubber | 4 |
| Heavy warpflamer | 23 |
| Helbrute plasma cannon | 30 |
| Hellfyre missile rack | 22 |
| Inferno bolt pistol | 1 |
| Inferno boltgun | 2 |
| Inferno combi-bolter | 3 |
| Krak grenades | 0 |
| Lascannon | 25 |
| Magma cutter | 16 |
| Missile launcher | 25 |
| Multi-melta | 27 |
| Plasma pistol | 7 |
| Predator autocannon | 40 |
| Reaper autocannon | 15 |
| Shotgun | 0 |
| Soulreaper cannon | 15 |
| Twin heavy bolter | 17 |
| Twin heavy flamer | 34 |
| Twin lascannon | 50 |
| Warpflame pistol | 7 |
| Warpflamer | 15 |

## MELEE WEAPONS

| WEAPON | POINTS PER WEAPON |
|---|---|
| Betentacled maw | 0 |
| Brutal assault weapon | 0 |
| Chainsword | 0 |
| Daemon jaws | 8 |
| Daemonic axe | 10 |
| Defiler claws | 0 |
| Defiler scourge | 12 |
| Divining spear | 1 |
| Enormous claws | 0 |
| Force stave | 8 |
| Force sword | 8 |
| Helbrute fist (single/pair) | 40/50 |
| Helbrute hammer | 52 |
| Heldrake claws | 17 |
| Hellforged sword | 10 |
| Hideous mutations | 0 |
| Lasher tendrils | 12 |
| Malefic talons (one set/two sets) | 0/10 |
| Maulerfiend fists | 0 |
| Power scourge | 43 |
| Power sword | 4 |
| Tzaangor blades | 0 |

## OTHER WARGEAR

| WARGEAR | POINTS PER ITEM |
|---|---|
| Brayhorn | 10 |
| Daemonic Icon | 15 |
| Familiar | 9 |
| Icon of Flame | 5 |
| Instrument of Chaos | 10 |

# TACTICAL OBJECTIVES

Even when they fought in the Great Crusade, the Thousand Sons were renowned for their devastating style of warfare, and they have maintained and perfected these tactics for more than ten millennia. They are at once implacable and adaptable; guided by the shifting tides of battle and yet unerring in their malefic desire for victory.

If your army is led by a **THOUSAND SONS** Warlord, these Tactical Objectives replace the Capture and Control Tactical Objectives (numbers 11-16) in the *Warhammer 40,000* rulebook. If a mission uses Tactical Objectives, players use the normal rules for using Tactical Objectives with the following exception: when a Thousand Sons player generates a Capture and Control objective (numbers 11-16), they instead generate the corresponding Thousand Sons Tactical Objective, as shown below. Other Tactical Objectives (numbers 21-66) are generated normally.

| D66 | TACTICAL OBJECTIVE |
|-----|--------------------|
| 11 | Ritual Slaughter |
| 12 | Psychic Supremacy |
| 13 | Vengeance Long Awaited |
| 14 | Arcane Rite |
| 15 | The Wrath of Magnus |
| 16 | Power of the Cabal |

## 11 — RITUAL SLAUGHTER — *Thousand Sons*

*The letting of blood is a powerful ingredient of fell rituals – spill it to Tzeentch's liking and reap the rewards.*

Score 1 victory point if at least nine enemy models were destroyed by units from your army during this turn.

## 12 — PSYCHIC SUPREMACY — *Thousand Sons*

*The sons of Prospero have long been masters of the empyrean – those who would rival their supremacy must have their works undone.*

Score 1 victory point if you made a successful Deny the Witch test during this turn.

## 13 — VENGEANCE LONG AWAITED — *Thousand Sons*

*The Thousand Sons have waited for millennia to avenge the wrongs of the Horus Heresy – now that reckoning is at hand.*

Score 1 victory point if at least one enemy unit was destroyed by units from your army during this turn. Score D3 victory points instead if at least one **IMPERIUM** unit was destroyed by units from your army during this turn.

## 14 — ARCANE RITE — *Thousand Sons*

*The land itself contains great power – for this geomantic rite to be complete, the battlefield must belong to the Thousand Sons.*

Score D3 victory points if you control at least one objective marker and your opponent controls no objective markers at the end of this turn.

## 15 — THE WRATH OF MAGNUS — *Thousand Sons*

*It is not enough to merely slay the enemy – they must be overcome in mind, body and spirit for Magnus' work to be complete.*

Score D3 victory points if at least one enemy unit was destroyed by units from your army during the Psychic phase of this turn.

## 16 — POWER OF THE CABAL — *Thousand Sons*

*Make Tzeentch's will manifest in realspace.*

Whilst this Tactical Objective is active, keep a tally of the number of psychic powers you successfully resolve during the Psychic phase each turn. At the end of the first turn in which you successfully resolved at least two psychic powers, score 1 victory point for every two psychic powers successfully resolved in that turn (to a maximum of 6 victory points).